THE FORTUNES OF WAR

THE FORTUNES

Four Great Battles

of World War II

by Andrew A. Rooney

OF WAR

LITTLE, BROWN AND COMPANY

Boston   Toronto

LIBRARY OF CONGRESS CATALOG CARD NO. 62-9550

First edition .

Published simultaneously in Canada
by Little, Brown & Company (Canada) Limited

PRINTED IN THE UNITED STATES OF AMERICA

Introduction, 1

TARAWA, *5*

STALINGRAD, *49*

D-DAY, *115*

THE BULGE, *192*

THE FORTUNES OF WAR

THERE HAS BEEN a great deal written about war, because war seems to make more interesting reading than peace. It would appear now, in the 1960s, that people writing about the kind of battles that have attracted readers will have to keep digging back into past wars for material. It doesn't seem likely that great armies will ever engage each other man to man, plane to plane or ship to ship again. Future wars are apt to be a good deal less interesting and more final.

War is often more interesting to read about than peace, for several reasons. Adventure makes good reading and there is something adventurous about the imminence of death. Death is always imminent in a war. Men themselves are more interesting at war, too. A man lives most of his life at half-throttle, using only a portion of his muscles, his brains and his emotions. War, being the ultimate competition, often calls forth qualities a man has never had occasion to see in himself before. He accomplishes physical feats he did not know his body was capable of, and thinks of things with both an ingenuity and a depth that were not called for in peace.

Books about war fall into two categories. The first is the straight history, the big picture—what happened to nations and armies. The second is the story of individuals at war, the details of what they did—their bravery and cowardice. This book attempts to combine the two. The material for books about war can be got from firsthand experience, from talking to people who were there, or from others' books about it. The material here comes from all three sources.

No one who was there is ever satisfied with someone else's story of a battle. It just does not seem to be the way it really was. The best a writer can do is try to get the facts in order and put them down in the spirit of the way things seemed to be, without relying too much on the synthetic particular which has become so popular. The facts of war seem dramatic enough.

There has always been a lot of general talk about peace in the world; but the specific talk has been about war. The general talk suggests war is horrible, and the specific talk indicates it is sometimes a wild and glorious adventure. This is partly because those for whom it was specifically most horrible are dead and cannot speak for their side of it. Governments talk as though wars were always undesirable—and act as though they were not. This is partly because no one has ever been able to total up the good and the evil that have come from wars and compare the balances. The talk about permanent peace presupposes that war is always bad; but that has not been clearly established.

It is clear that killing does not come naturally to a man, and it is difficult to get him to the point where he will do it for any reason. It's been made easier for him over the years, though. With the exception of a few bayonet skirmishes, the killing in both World War I and World War II was less personal than it had ever been. An infantryman did not see the look on the face of a man he shot with a rifle at two hundred yards, nor did he know the man had a picture of his wife and children in his breast pocket. The pilot of a plane that dropped bombs on a city did not usually have a conscience burdened with the deaths of several hundred people below him, because he was never sure he had killed anyone.

Because war became less personal, and because very few people did the actual fighting and dying in war anyway, more men returned with pleasant memories than with unpleasant ones. Even some of those who fought but did not die recall more of the adventure than of the misery. They forget the long, dull, tedious days of nothing.

Some men who were lonely and insecure as peaceful civilians found companionship and pleasure in having a common objective with other men. They remembered this. If a man had natural aggressive instincts he had curbed in his normal society, he could indulge his aggressions to his heart's content in a war. He could even kill with nothing but approval from the others in his group. If he had these aggressive instincts, and was properly convinced that he was fighting for a just cause, he got both a sense of freedom from conventional restrictions and a sense of satisfaction that he was doing a good thing. This was a pleasant adventure for him.

These pleasant memories some men bring back contribute

to the world's continued acceptance of war as a state to be considered.

It should be made clear in any book about war that there is almost nothing pleasant about it. The truism is true: war is hell. And the hell of it should not be diminished in favor of its adventure.

Fortunes of War is based, in outline, on four half-hour television documentaries produced for the CBS News television series, *The Twentieth Century*. Full use was made of the enormous amount of research material collected by the staff of executive producer Burton Benjamin. Their help was important, but conclusions, where they are drawn, and opinions, where they are expressed, are the writer's. The pictures have been taken from the files of *The Twentieth Century*, but because single frames taken from motion pictures are not usually as satisfactory in reproduction as still photos, these were augmented. The services of Julius North of *The Twentieth Century* staff were invaluable in preparation of the pictures. In many cases pictures do not exactly fit the narration, because, during many of the most dangerous and therefore most dramatic battle situations, it was not practical for photographers to be standing around taking pictures. Robert Capa, the greatest war photographer, was an exception: he landed with the United States troops on D-Day and shot eleven rolls of film. All but seven pictures were ruined in the dark room and as a result there are few pictures of D-Day that illustrate anything that happened during the height of that battle.

In addition to Burton Benjamin, the writer also thanks Miss Barbara Sapinsley of *The Twentieth Century* staff, who helped in the picture selection, and Murray Benson of CBS, who was instrumental in bringing the author and the publisher together for the development of this book.

TARAWA

NO ONE KNOWS who he was. He came wading in with a rifle high over his head. When he hit the beach he was one of four left from the group of twenty Marines dumped on the coral reef six hundred yards offshore by the tiny blue Higgins boat. The machine gun that had dropped the others into the shallow lagoon dead, or wounded to drown with seventy-five pounds on their backs, was still firing as he fell to the beach.

The Marine lay still for perhaps five minutes. His clothes started to turn light as they dried in the hot sun, except for a sticky red splotch seeping through his shirt high on his left shoulder. He raised his head. The Japanese machine gun was concealed in a nest one hundred feet to his right and four feet above him, behind the barricade of coconut logs that formed a seawall the length of the beach.

The Marine looked back. He saw men from a second Higgins boat pile out to start the long wade in. As they came closer machine-gun bullets kicked up the water around them. Heads— then rifles—sank into the riled waters until there were only half a dozen Marines coming on.

The man on the beach, his shoulder oozing blood, got to his knees, crouched and ran for the log barrier. He pulled himself up to the sandy plateau four feet above the beach, and Marines behind saw him work his way laterally along across the top of the log barrier. They lost sight of him behind a tangle of brush as he moved slightly inland. Suddenly there were wild shouts in two languages, a hysterical burst of machine-gun fire and a grenade explosion.

Two Japanese machine-gunners were blown apart and a Marine ten feet from their position lay in two pieces, cut through the middle by a last burst of fire.

The Marines offshore waded the last two hundred yards safely, never knowing why the raking machine-gun fire had stopped—and no one who knew had time to tell them.

AN ATOLL IS A CRESCENT-SHAPED ISLAND or series of islands and the lagoon they shelter. For four days beginning November 20, 1943, the smallest and bloodiest of the great battles of World

War II took place on and in the waters around Betio, the largest bead in the necklace of islands forming Tarawa Atoll. The battle's plan and its progress are known in intimate detail because it was small, but in the perspective of history the island itself hardly matters. Tarawa is important because of the extremes of courage men found in themselves and because of the warmth generated by a story that illustrates, with rare clarity, that man cares for his fellow man. It holds out hope that men have within themselves untapped wells of love and unselfishness.

For all its tactical unimportance, the story of individual heroism and mass bravery at Tarawa can be told only through a narrative of the battle.

THE SITUATION

When the United States entered the war in 1941, it did not have the strength to fight two major wars simultaneously. It could not apply pressure to the Japanese in the Pacific and fight the Germans in Europe. During the period when men were being trained to fight and the weapons they were to fight with were being made, the United States concentrated most of what strength it had in Europe. The Japanese, however, could not be ignored. They had systematically acquired islands from Australia to Alaska and established strong bases over thousands of miles of the Pacific. For two years, frustrated Pacific commanders worked with what they could get to hold off the creeping Japanese offensive.

On June 3, 1943, the Japanese bombed Dutch Harbor in the Aleutian Islands from carrier-based planes. Two weeks later Japanese troops moved into the islands of Kiska and Attu. The Aleutians loop out more than one thousand miles into the Pacific off the Southern end of Alaska, and while Attu is at the western end of the string of islands, it is fewer than 2500 air miles from Portland, Oregon. Dutch Harbor, the United States base which they had attacked, is only 1500. The war was getting too close for the comfort of Americans on the West Coast.

Admiral Chester W. Nimitz had been put in command of

a huge area including the Solomon Islands in the South Pacific, the Gilberts, of which Tarawa Atoll was a part, the Marianas, the Carolines and the Marshalls; and in the North, those nearest the United States mainland, the Aleutians. General Douglas Mac-Arthur was put in command of the Southwest Pacific Theater—Australia, New Guinea, the Philippines and the Netherlands East Indies.

As American strength doubled and tripled, more men and machines were sent into the war in the Pacific, which was pressed with power, skill and ingenuity. Like a man jumping from rock to rock in a shallow creek, United States forces jumped from island to island, to move close enough for an attack on Japan. They bombed and shelled, moved troops in, established naval and air bases, caught their balance and jumped again.

Americans on the West Coast breathed easier after Attu was cleared of Japanese in a small, nasty, three-week fight through the cold, fog-shrouded hills of that volcanic island. That fight began on June 2, 1943. Six weeks after Attu was cleared, a combined force of Canadians and Americans went into Kiska, a larger Japanese base. This attack was preceded by heavy naval shelling. It had been anticipated that Kiska would not be taken as quickly as Attu had been: every man bristling with equipment, the landing force went ashore.

It turned out to be a joke of war. Under cover of the Aleutian fog the Japanese had moved in a fleet of sixteen ships to evacuate five thousand men. United States bombs and shells landed on a ghost base. The fighting men felt relieved, but somehow cheated, and for the rest of the war the United States Marines never quite got over half-hoping, half-fearing that their next invasion would be like Kiska.

By November 1943, Americans had battled their way onto most of the Solomons, through Guadalcanal, and MacArthur had started his campaign in New Guinea. The next logical move was the Gilberts, those coral islands stretched out along the equator twenty-five hundred miles southwest of Hawaii, eleven hundred

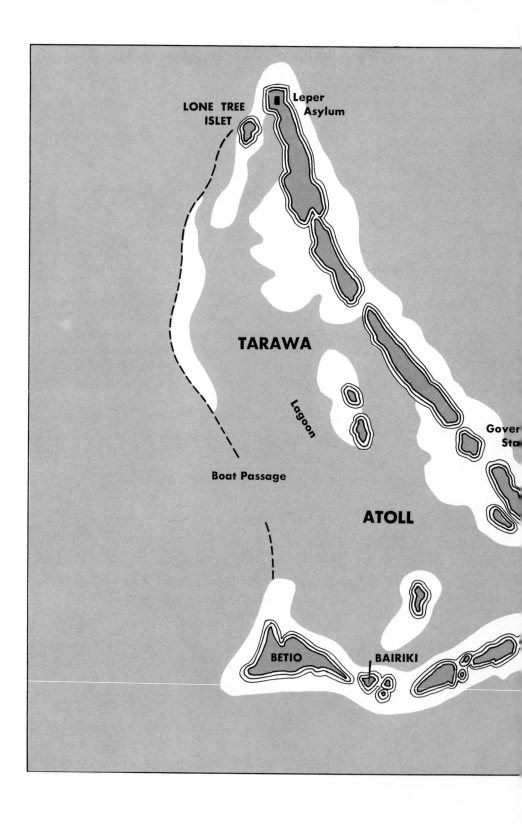

miles northeast of Guadalcanal and twenty-nine hundred miles southeast of Tokyo. As far as the American Marines were concerned, the Gilberts were very damn close to nowhere. For forty-nine years before the Japanese moved in on Christmas Day, 1941, the island group had been occupied by the British.

Tarawa Atoll is a badly shaped V about eighteen miles long on its eastern side and twelve on its southern. It might be called a triangle, except that what there is of its third, western side is composed of twelve and a half miles of coral reefs, most of which appear at low tide. There are two deep-water openings into the sheltered lagoon.

There are forty-seven lumps of land in the atoll, many of them not big enough to be called islands. Betio, the biggest, is on the extreme end of the southern leg of the V. It is roughly three miles long, one thousand yards wide at its widest—a total of two hundred and ninety acres. Robert Sherrod, a *Life* correspondent at the time of the invasion, described Betio as being shaped like a bird. The picture is one of a woodpecker, perhaps, sitting on a perch, wings folded. The head is the end of the island, and the tail trails off towards the island next to it, Bairiki.

THE DEFENSES

What made Betio the object of this attack was its excellent airstrip; what made Betio unique was its fortifications. Gun and man per square foot, it was the most heavily fortified island in the world. Samuel Eliot Morison, in Volume VII of his *History of United States Naval Operations*, said, "No military historian who viewed these defenses could recall an instance of a small island's having been so well prepared for an attack. Corregidor was an open town by comparison."

The Japanese had done everything that time, effort and ingenuity could accomplish to protect Tarawa. They left no stone unturned if turning the stone would offer any help to the island's defense. They varied their defense to fit the geography.

In the water off the beaches least protected by the coral reefs offshore—that is, where the reefs were covered by more

than twenty feet of water at high tide—they built pyramid-shaped concrete obstacles. Steel bars like railroad track were set into the concrete to protrude at odd angles. These obstacles, barely above water at high tide, were put close enough together so that no boat or amphibious vehicle could pass between any two of them. In front of other stretches of beach the Japanese had planted formidable coconut-log barriers. Ringing the island was a double fence of tangled barbed wire. It was an insurmountable barrier that had to be surmounted.

Around the edge of the island they had dug a moat. The steep sides of this wide ditch made it an effective tank trap. Just behind this, at the beach's high-water mark, they had put up a strange wall of coconut tree stumps, three to five feet high.

Within these protective rings, the Japanese built protective structures for themselves and their weapons. The concrete for these blockhouses was poured over a skeletal form of steel. When the concrete hardened, it was covered with wood, as if the Japs had been building a coconut-log cabin.

Many of these, designed as gun placements, were built partially below ground. After the coconut logs were in place the whole top of the structure was covered with eight or ten feet of sand. Marines were to learn that sand and the stringy, fibrous coconut logs absorb bombs and bullets more effectively than concrete. If the Japanese at Hiroshima had lived in anything like these Tarawa fortifications, it is probable that few would have been killed when the Bomb dropped.

Where there were gaps in any of the barriers in the water, they were deliberate—designed to funnel attackers into a channel most effectively covered by heavy gunfire. There were four eight-inch guns on Betio, any one of which was capable of sinking any ship afloat. There were ten other heavy coastal defense guns. There were also forty-three antiaircraft guns which could always be depressed and used against ground or water targets, and a total of about ninety machine guns in Japanese hands.

"The Americans," said Japanese commander Admiral Keiji Shibasaki, "could not take Tarawa with a million men in a hundred years."

JUST BEFORE

On November 1, the 2nd Marine Division sailed out of Oriental Bay and Marines on deck looked back at the hills behind Wellington, New Zealand, with affection and good memories. They had gone there to lick their wounds after the fight for Guadalcanal, and had found a friendly home.

The official and elaborately contrived story was that they were headed for landing maneuvers at Hawke Bay, New Zealand. No one knew whether Japanese informants took the bait, but the way things worked out it was as if the United States had told the Japanese where they were coming and when—and then came there. No Marines were fooled by the sham Hawke Bay maneuver orders. They'd been on maneuvers and they'd played for keeps. They sensed this one wasn't going to be a practice session.

The troop carriers were combat-loaded. Each unit—single fighting Marine, platoon, company, battalion, landing team—was packed aboard to give it maximum independence. They were ready to come off fighting.

As the convoy moved into the open sea, the men settled down to those things men always settle down to on dreary long voyages to destination unknown. They slept, played cards, drank coffee, cleaned weapons that weren't dirty, and wrote letters which, in many cases, were not ripped open by anxious mothers until their sons were dead.

In small groups they sang old songs and composed new ones. Any tune they all knew was subject to parody and they all knew the Artillery's "Caisson Song." One parody of that moved from ship to ship over the same mysterious communication system that carries a rumor instantaneously to all members of any fighting force:

OVER SEA, OVER FOAM
WISH TO CHRIST THAT WE WERE HOME,
BUT THE TRANSPORTS GO SAILING ALONG.
IN AND OUT, NEAR AND FAR,
WONDER WHERE THE HELL WE ARE,
AS THE TRANSPORTS GO SAILING ALONG.
SO IT'S HO HO HUM, ICELAND HERE WE COME,

OR MAYBE THE AZORES OR DAKAR:

BUT WHERE'ER IT BE, WE'LL GET NO LIBERTY,

AS THE TRANSPORTS GO SAILING ALONG.

The convoy plowed south through the Pacific waters, additional cruisers and destroyers appearing at its outer edges, dropping into the pattern and becoming part of it. The battleships *Maryland, Colorado* and *Tennessee* pulled into line, their sixteen-inch guns lending authority to the growing armada.

On the morning of November 15, ship commanders received the word to open their sealed orders. Task Force Commander Rear Admiral Harry Hill sent this message to every ship in the convoy:

> GIVE ALL HANDS THE GENERAL PICTURE OF THE PROJECTED OPERATION AND FURTHER DETAILS TO ALL WHO SHOULD HAVE THIS IN EXECUTION OF DUTIES. THIS IS THE FIRST AMERICAN ASSAULT OF A STRONGLY DEFENDED ATOLL AND, WITH NORTHERN ATTACK AND COVERING FORCES, THE LARGEST PACIFIC OPERATION TO DATE.

Now, though knowing the name of their target—the island fortress of Betio, Tarawa Atoll—2nd Marine Division still knew very little. There was no marked effect on the card games or the letters home, although the bull sessions turned more often from talk of women to arguments about the best place to get hit. Most preferred a clean bullet wound in the thigh or the fleshy part of the upper arm.

While the sixteen transports filled with fighting Marines were steaming steadily toward their target, with their huge escort of Navy support ships, Betio was an ant's-nest of activity. The Japanese knew what was coming—it was a question of which side of the island the Marines would come from. On successive days the Japanese were hit by four hundred carrier- and land-based Navy planes and by big B–24 bombers of the Seventh Air Force. On November 18 the air attack was supplemented by a surface bombardment from three heavy cruisers and two destroyers lying offshore. The Japanese knew this was no hit-and-run raid. They

scurried to make last-minute defense preparations for what they were already confident was an impregnable fort.

The night of November 19 was hot and sticky. The ships were no longer moving fast enough to create their own breeze. In the holds below, Marines had stopped talking except for an occasional mirthless joke. They were not fearless, but they were not afraid. Many went to their bunks that night thinking it might be their last night on earth. The thought had sometimes seemed to save them from the fact, although this night many who thought it must have been right.

What air there was below decks that night was crackling with tension. Those who could sleep were brought to their feet by the Marine buglers aboard the ships at 12:45 A.M. Breakfast was at 1 A.M.—steak, eggs, fried potatoes.

The transports were scheduled to be in position off Tarawa at 3:20 A.M. They were not, and this was the first of a series of mistakes that were to make the landing more difficult. The transports were ordered to move north to their proper location. Each transport had at its heels a yapping pack of smaller boats designed to carry the men to the island. The move was accomplished, but in the darkness and confusion many of the smaller boats lost their mother ships.

With the transports in position, Marines started over the side, down the rope ladders into the small, powerful Higgins boats and LCVPs. Betio was quiet. If the Japanese had seen the great fleet, they were holding their fire.

At 4:41 A.M. the Japanese sent a red star cluster whistling into the sky over Tarawa. In itself, it was a harmless firecracker, but it alerted every Japanese soldier that the time had come.

Half an hour later, still in the gray-dark of a Pacific early morning, Japanese shore batteries opened fire. If there ever had been a secret about the invasion it was a secret no longer, and the *Maryland* and *Colorado* opened up with the belching fire and

Into the boats.

terrifying boom of their sixteen-inch guns. The island had been marked off in blocks on maps, and gunnery officers went about putting heavy shells into each checkerboard square. Japanese shells splashed into the ocean all around the battleships but there were no hits.

During this time Marines were pouring overboard into their landing craft—if the landing craft had stayed with its troop carrier. After a half-hour of shelling, a Cease Fire order was issued. There was now enough light to allow for one final pre-landing air strike before Marines heading for shore in small boats got close enough to be endangered by their own bombers. Simultaneous air and naval strikes were impractical because shellbursts sent so much smoke and dirt into the air that pilots couldn't see their targets.

Had the air strike come as ordered, the invasion might still have come off on time despite the confusion of lost landing craft and transports that were not in their designated positions in relation to the shore. But the air strike did not come, and for half an hour the ships floated helplessly, holding their fire while the Japanese artillery threw shells at them.

In the small boats much of the landing force was splashing its way toward shore several miles off. Control of a ship-to-shore operation such as this is in the hands of the United States Navy until the invaders touch solid ground. It must have been a hard-pressed Admiral Hill who ordered resumption of naval fire when the planes did not arrive. It was his responsibility to get the men ashore. Ten minutes after the battleships, cruisers and destroyers had started firing again, the planes arrived.

Both air and naval fire helped. The biggest of the Japanese guns were no longer firing by eight o'clock, but the landing deadline, H-hour, 8:30 A.M., was obviously not going to be met. Hundreds of Marines made the difficult transfer from LCVPs into what the Japanese called "the little boat with wheels," the amphibious tractor, shortened by Marines to "amtrac." It had been determined that if the tide was low and the reefs bare, none of the other landing craft could get into the lagoon. The amtracs could trundle over the coral reefs and paddle to shore. All the landing craft were making slow progress, and despite the communications complications, H-hour was delayed until 8:45. Ten minutes later, with the invading Marines still well out from the beaches, H-hour was delayed until 9 A.M.

Precise times didn't matter much to the Marines going in. They couldn't move any faster than the boats carrying them, and they were the reason for everything else being there. But delaying H-hour meant a snarl of messages from command battleships to other fighting vessels, from battleships to transport ships, from transport ships to landing boats, from landing boats to airplanes and all back again—and to each other. A bomb or a shell kills friend or enemy alike and co-ordinated fire and bombing support was important to protect Marines. It was also important that the siege last until the last possible minute. Men duck when fired at, and while the fire from the ships or from low-flying planes was intense, the Japanese would not expose themselves.

If Admiral Hill and General Julian C. Smith, 2nd Marine Division commander, were sick with worry over the apparent disorganization, men moving towards shore in small boats had a more physical problem. The sea was rough, and the square-nosed landing boats bounced into waves that threw the small boats wildly over the water. Sheets of ocean spread over the open boats. The trip was a nightmare. It would seem as though those embarking on a highly dangerous mission would be immune to the minor ills that afflict men under normal circumstances, but the fact was that many of the men became violently seasick.

The sun rose on smoldering Betio Island at 6:12 the morning of November 20, 1943. An officer of the Royal New Zealand Navy who had plied these waters on merchant ships during peacetime was now aboard the United States minesweeper *Pursuit*, as pilot. It was followed by the minesweeper *Requisite*. These two small warships made their way through the narrow deep-water channel, about six miles from Betio, into the lagoon. When shore batteries opened fire on them as they steamed up the lagoon towards Betio and prepared to start the smoke-pots designed to screen the landing craft, they asked for supporting fire from two destroyers

waiting just outside. They got it. These destroyers, *Ringgold* and *Dashiell,* along with the two minesweepers, are the only elements of the naval force to which the Marines will give anything more than reluctant credit. These tough little ships came through the gap and at point-blank range opened fire on Japanese shore positions with great effectiveness. They were as good as ten tanks on the beach. Five minutes after the *Ringgold* entered the shallow lagoon, a five-inch Japanese shell crashed into the starboard engine room. The next instant a second shell hit a torpedo tube, glanced off into the ship's hospital room and penetrated to the emergency radio room. The *Ringgold* never stopped firing.

At 8:54 A.M. the order once again went out for all naval and air bombardment to cease. H-hour was 9 A.M., and because ships offshore were not sight-firing, six minutes was considered a minimum margin of safety for troops going in. It was more than twenty minutes before the first men reached the beach; and during these crucial minutes they were without support fire except from the blessed *Ringgold* and *Dashiell.* Because these two ships could see what they were shooting at, they alone were exempt from the Cease Fire order.

Many of the landing craft bringing men towards shore were still beyond the range of small arms and machine-gun fire, but AP (anti-personnel) shells were bursting overhead. An AP shell is timed to explode over its target. The shell casing is blown into thousands of small, viciously irregular missiles which kill men below as effectively as a hundred snipers hanging from the clouds. The first Marines died this way.

At 9 A.M. the picture was this:

(1) Five to six miles offshore, a fighting fleet including three battleships, five cruisers and seven destroyers. They were not firing, because the landing parties were too close to the beaches.

*The men fight singly
and in small groups.*

(2) Under the protective cover of the warships, sixteen troop transport ships, many of which had just disgorged their passengers into small landing craft. In addition, one transport loaded with medium tanks, its crew working feverishly to unload the tanks into bouncing landing boats at its side.

(3) Overhead, within two minutes of any target they were asked by radio to hit, F6Fs (Grumman Hellcats), and SB2Cs (Helldivers). Like the ships, the planes were holding their fire.

(4) In the lagoon, firing point-blank at Japanese positions, two destroyers.

(5) On the water heading for Tarawa in four types of landing craft, three battalions, about 2500 Marines. They were bucking towards the coral reef which protected the lagoon in square-bowed Higgins boats, LCVPs (Landing Craft, Vehicle, Personnel), LCMs (Landing Craft, Medium), and LVTs (Landing Vehicle, Tracked). About one mile out, spent machine-gun and rifle fire began to ping off their metal sides. Worse, word reached the small landing craft that the tide was unexpectedly low. The coral reef was barely covered with rippling water. Nothing but amtracs could take men across it.

(6) On the island of Betio, 4707 heavily armed Japanese dug in tight. Their island fortress was a smoldering ruin on the surface, but beneath their steel-log-sand strongpoints, they were alive and ready.

THE LANDING

The first Marines touched dry sand at about 9:10.

The first three waves came in the amphibious landing tanks. Eight sank or were blown out of the water on the way in, and most of their fifteen men lost. The situation was not bad for the moment, though. The first battalion reached shore with relatively few casualties. Two of the amtracs found a hole in the seawall and pushed inland toward the airfield taxi strip that came close to the edge of the island at that point. The men who landed on the beach directly in front of the two destroyers made out best.

It was 9:30 before the true difficulty of the situation became apparent. Most of the amtracs that made the beach on their original drive had been damaged. Bullets, which had bounced off their thin metal skins farther out, penetrated now. As the amtracs dropped their passengers, spun on the sand and started back for a second load of Marines, fifteen of them (of a total of eighty-six) disappeared in the deeper waters of the lagoon.

Out on the reef perhaps fifteen hundred men who had come from the transports in the larger landing craft were trapped. Nothing but amtracs could cross the coral barrier. Many men started wading the five hundred yards, rifles high, through withering machine-gun fire. The water varied in depth from zero to twenty feet, but the bottom was not always regular and bomb and shell craters pocked the lagoon's floor. Many Marines drowned as they stepped into ten or fifteen feet of water with seventy-five pounds of fighting equipment strapped to their backs.

The beach was divided into three areas code-named Red Beach 1, Red Beach 2 and Red Beach 3. The men on Red 2 and Red 3 were under direct machine-gun fire.

"It was like being in the middle of a pool table with no pockets," Sergeant Welles Grey said.

By ten o'clock the situation was desperate. Marines were dying the length of the beach and the width of the lagoon. Many of them fell as they pulled themselves out of the water, so that the high tide was marked by irregular rows of Marine bodies. Dozens of them died horribly on the barbed-wire entanglements in the shallow waters off the beach. They were burned as shells crashed through the gas-tank sides of their amtracs and turned them into instant infernos. Bullets are unselective; the Japanese were not listening when the Marines talked of where they'd prefer to be hit. Bullets ripped off faces, testicles, shattered knee caps or whistled clean through a chest—details of war that don't often find their way into history books.

Units became separated, well-laid plans were lost, and it was every man for himself and the man next to him and the man down the beach. They were held together only by the common determination to move in and wipe out the Japanese firing at them. The ability of these Americans to fight intelligently without formal organization won the battle of Tarawa as it won so many other battles of World War II.

Colonel Merritt Edson said afterwards: "It is my opinion that the reason we won this show was the ability of junior officers and noncoms to take command of small groups of six to eight or ten men, regardless of where those men came from, and to organize and lead them as a fighting team."

He might have added that often two privates made a fighting team of themselves.

The highest-ranking Japanese soldier to survive the battle, Sergeant Kiyoshi Ohta, has said since: "I ordered my soldiers not to fire until the landing boats were within two hundred meters. I thought we wouldn't be able to destroy the great power of the enemy unless we caught them on the beach and destroyed them there at once."

It appeared as though the Marines might be destroyed. The attack had been laid out in infinite detail. But there was no plan for retreat. With admirable arrogance, Marine commanders had not considered the possibility. There was not now, and never had been, any thought of withdrawal.

While Marine landing teams were fighting their way up onto the beaches and clawing their way to the coconut-log wall twenty feet from the water, a special unit of thirty-four hand-picked riflemen and engineers, led by Lieutenant William D. Hawkins, was accomplishing the most important and dangerous mission of the initial attack. Tarawa was dominated by a pier that jutted seven hundred and fifty yards out into the deeper water of the lagoon, providing a place for sheltered unloading of supply ships. Invasion plans called for landings on either side of the pier, but if the pier itself was not cleared of Japanese it was apparent they would sweep the beaches with machine-gun fire.

Hawkins became a Marine legend in less than forty-eight hours. At about nine o'clock, fifteen minutes before the amtracs touched bottom on the beaches, Hawkins and his thirty-four men reached the end of the pier. While the scout-snipers rattled bullets off the outer Japanese position, Lieutenant A. G. Leslie, Hawkins, and four engineers moved along the pier. Once within

range, Leslie opened the valve on his flame thrower and burned out the enemy gunners. (Unfortunately, the wooden beams and decking caught fire and burned a fifty-foot gap in the pier.)

As soon as Hawkins's scout-sniper platoon had cleared the pier, they moved inland over the seawall. No one knows how many Japanese they killed, or how many machine-gun holes they cleared out. Every few hours someone would see "Hawk" dash back over to the beach side of the seawall. Always he was after more ammunition. On that first day he was caught by half a dozen bits of shrapnel which didn't slow him down. He directed his platoon with a fury that never slackened. On the second day, Hawk caught a bullet fairly high on one shoulder and started losing blood. He kept going until later the second day, when another bullet went through his other shoulder nearer the body cavity; but he still refused to be evacuated.

"I came here to kill Japs; I didn't come here to be evacuated," he said to medical corpsmen trying to persuade him to retire.

"He's a madman," one man said who had been over the sea-wall with him. "He cleaned out six machine-gun nests with two to six Japs in each nest. I'll never forget the picture of him standing on that amtrac, riding around with a million bullets a minute whistling by his ears, just shooting Japs. I never saw such a man in my life."

It seemed for a while as though Hawk would end up as the greatest living Marine hero when the battle was over. The cold facts of war are seldom any help to dramatic construction. Lieutenant William Deane Hawkins of El Paso, Texas, died on the beach from loss of blood during the second night.

Heroism is a word that does not stand close inspection. It was suggested by one Marine officer that no medals should be asked for any of the Marines at Tarawa because there was no one who could be left out. His contention was that they were all heroes. They were not all heroes—if by the word the user means fearless. Some men are less sensitive to danger than others, but if there were any unafraid Marines on Tarawa, they were thoughtless, not brave. Most of them openly confessed fear and

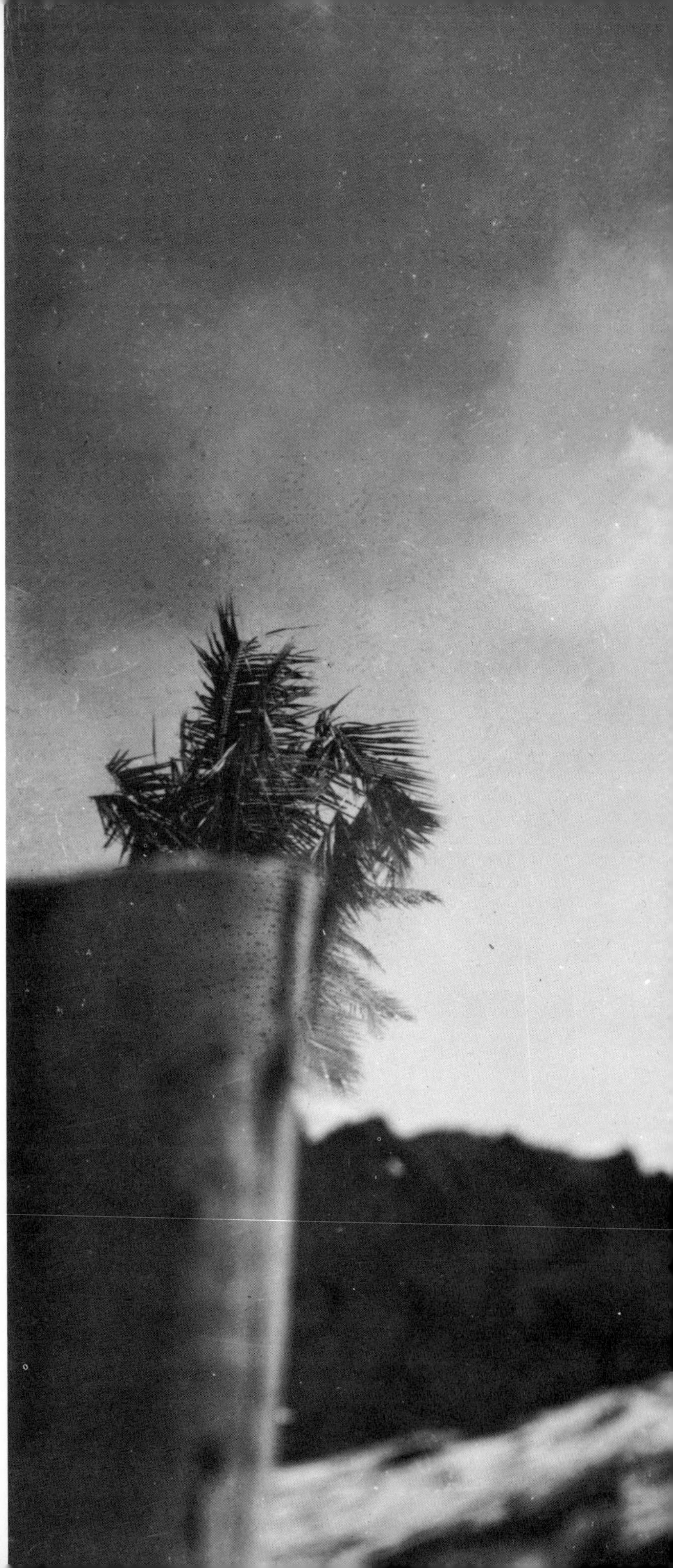

those Marine commanders who suggest that the men took Tarawa because they were not afraid to die degrade the virtue that drove them on. Marines continued to push forward because the lives of other men depended on their doing it.

Not all the Marines on Tarawa were heroic. Many of them, coming in past the area protected by the concrete pyramids set out in the water, took refuge behind these. Ahead of them the waters were red with the blood of men dead or dying in the water. Who is to say whether their action was cowardice or good sense? But there was no sitting and waiting for long. Someone had to go get every Japanese gunner. If ten men exposed themselves and rushed a position, it was a success when three of them made it and eliminated the enemy.

One of the tragedies of battle is that the bravest go first— and are the first to go. The greatest single American weapon in war has been the smart, tough, aggressive platoon sergeant willing to lead his small handful of men anywhere. At Tarawa, as elsewhere, it was the invaluable leaders, the platoon sergeants and the fighting junior officers, who were cut down first as they led their men into gunfire.

By 11 A.M. Colonel David M. Shoup, in overall command of the landing force, had managed to get to a somewhat protected position on one side of the pier near the beach. It was hardly an ideal command post. Shoup, with an aide and a sergeant with a radio strapped to his back, stood hip-deep in water trying to direct a battle over which he had no control. What he needed was more men, artillery and tanks. Fourteen tanks had started in off the transport *Ashland*. A few medium landing craft with tanks had cleared the reef. But as they came across the lagoon, the Japanese opened fire on them with artillery. Several of the LCMs went down with their tanks and men. Loaded with tanks, they drew about four feet of water. When the rest of the LCMs scraped coral a few hundred feet offshore, they dropped their ramps; the tanks rolled out into the lagoon and most of these reached the beach.

Many of the lighters carrying tanks in from the *Ashland*

could not clear the reef and were unloaded on that coral obstacle as far as one thousand yards from shore. These Sherman tanks started the long wade towards shore with water often reaching their gun turrets. Because of the potholes in the floor of the lagoon, each tank, somewhat immune itself to small-arms fire, had to be led by a Marine protected by nothing but his khaki shirt. These reconnaissance men planted flagged poles where they found holes too deep for a tank to negotiate. Many of these reconnaissance men were hit by machine-gun or rifle fire, but as soon as one dropped another Marine picked up the flag and forged on.

As the tanks rumbled in, the commanders of one group of six were faced with a dreadful decision. On the beach or in the shallow waters ahead of them were perhaps fifty dead or badly wounded Marines. The only other access was off around the outer end of a beach barrier. They do not print pictures of men who have been run over by tanks, but these tank commanders had seen the sight too often. Wheeling abruptly, the six tanks started parallel along the beach, still in two or three feet of water. As they reached the area that had been too deep for wading Marines, four of the six tanks dropped out of sight into a deep coral shelf. Two made it to the beach.

In a second group of tanks reaching land, only one, *China Gal*, survived. One dropped into a Japanese gasoline dump, trapping its crew in an instant hell. One was hit, later in the day, by an American dive-bomber; one dropped into an enemy shellhole and, while its crew was not hurt, it could not be extricated. Two, hit by enemy shells, caught fire. It went this way with these tanks until only *China Gal* was left to fight. Two tanks disabled on the beach did provide some sort of cover, and their machine guns were working—so they were of great help even though immobilized.

After the first toehold was gained by the original assault waves, there was almost no progress for several hours. Few of the men could move off the twenty yards of beach between the water and the seawall. The reef, the lagoon and the beach were cluttered with wrecked equipment and dead or dying men. Fewer than 1500 Marines were ashore, and those commanders who could

reach Colonel Shoup by radio or messenger reported: SITUATION DESPERATE. The only equipment on the beach was what the men had carried in on their backs. Ammunition was getting low, plasma for the bleeding was gone, and by this time everyone needed water. Of the original eighty-six amtracs, only a small handful were still running. Wading Marines were still being mowed down in clusters. Communications were fouled by wet radios that had not been too good dry; and, to further complicate the mess, they were having trouble in the radio room on the old battleship *Maryland,* from which Division General Julian Smith was to have directed the operation. The "Mary's" sixteen-inch guns had shaken loose her own teeth. When Shoup could not reach Julian Smith, he dispatched an aide to get back to one of the destroyers in the lagoon with orders to ask General Smith to send in anyone left on the ships who could fight. Julian Smith, in turn, had tried to contact Shoup about committing the reserve battalion, but none of these messages or the men carrying them got through.

By nightfall Colonel Shoup had moved his command post up behind a bombproof shelter inhabited by twenty Japanese. Marines along the beach tried to find some protection for themselves as the light faded. They dug shallow holes in the sand, huddled close up behind the seawall or found some protection behind a knocked-out tank or amtrac. Japanese fire became less frequent, although Japanese snipers lashed into the top fronds of coconut trees were still popping away sporadically. These snipers were hard to spot, because the Japanese had the cunning to provide them with a smokeless powder that left no telltale mark of their position.

The quiet of the night as darkness came was more terrifying than the noise of the day's battle. Everyone knew there would be a Japanese counterattack. During the day single Japanese soldiers had occasionally dashed from behind the seawall to throw a grenade at one of the approaching amtracs. There was no reason to think they would not be organized into groups for banzai attacks like that against the pitifully weak Marine positions on the beach. Every man's thoughts were his own that night; but no one slept, no one spoke and no one fired. Wounded Marines slowly turning white as blood dripped from the holes in their bodies did not whimper or groan. And the attack never came.

THE SECOND DAY

The second day began as the first had ended and from the sounds Marines knew the situation was unchanged. They knew what Japanese machine gun positions were still intact, what artillery was still picking away at landing boats in the lagoon, and they could tell that dead Japanese snipers, unable to fall from where they were tied in their tree hideouts, had been replaced. Every sound was meaningful; after a day in battle every soldier has true pitch. In war you fire as much at what you hear as at what you see. For this reason a soldier out of ammunition for his own weapon does not pick up the rifle of a dead enemy. Sounds mean everything in war, and as the last major reserve unit landed on the reef at 6:15 the morning of November 21 and started wading for shore, Marines on the beach heard a familiar noise from a new direction and turned to see a sickening sight.

The waves of Marines in the water between the reef and the beach could be seen clutching at themselves in anguish or dropping quickly beneath the surface. They were taking fire directly from the seawall and now from both flanks. It took a moment for the startled Marines on shore to grasp what was happening. During the night daring Japanese gunners had crept across the beach and out into the lagoon to infest the half-sunken tanks and half tracks. At one point along the beach a Japanese freighter that had gone down there three months before the invasion lay deep in sand but with her decks well above water. The Japanese had carried machine guns aboard, and from this position were decimating the Marine battalion in the water.

During almost an hour of panic more of these second-day Marine invaders were killed than in any battalion on D-Day. When Navy gunners on the *Ringgold* and *Dashiell* saw what was happening, they rattled direct and heavy fire into both the freighters and the abandoned Marine vehicles until the Japanese were silenced. They were not silenced until they were dead. It was the most enterprising single Japanese maneuver of the battle, and the most costly to the 2nd Marine Division.

Just before nine o'clock Colonel Shoup was near desperation. Things did not seem to be going well at all and with communication re-established he radioed:

> IMPERATIVE YOU LAND AMMUNITION, WATER, RATIONS AND MEDICAL SUPPLIES . . . AND EVACUATE CASUALTIES . . . SITUATION DOESN'T LOOK GOOD ASHORE.

There were no signs of any real progress inland, supplies and re-enforcements were not coming in any helpful amounts; and moreover Japanese resistance was still strong.

The temperature on the island rose above 110 degrees and the atoll began to reek of human bodies decaying in the merciless tropical sun. The gases generated in a bullet-riddled man bloat the body cavity and the pressure often forces gangrenous coils of entrails out any openings. No one who has ever seen it understands a child's fascination with playing soldier.

ROUTING THEM OUT

The tide of battle turned sometime during that second day. It was imperceptible at first to those on Betio, but by noon the waters in the lagoon had finally risen high enough so that Higgins boats and other landing craft could cross the water and discharge men, tanks, artillery and supplies on or near the beach itself. Somewhere around four o'clock that second afternoon, Colonel Shoup sent one of the classic war messages:

> CASUALTIES: MANY. PERCENTAGE DEAD: NOT KNOWN. COMBAT EFFICIENCY: WE ARE WINNING.

The Marines were winning. But many more were to die before the battle of Tarawa was won, and in many respects the hardest fighting was ahead.

The Japanese were holed up in five hundred large and small pillboxes. Many of them were determined to die rather than be captured. This determination is variously described in war—depending on whether those determined to die are with you or against you—as "bravery" or "fanaticism." Whichever it was with the Japanese, the Marines were ready to go along with it. In the first place, there was no good way to surrender. Marines who had seen companions fall on both sides of them were in no mood to ask Japanese who exposed themselves whether they'd had enough or not. In the second place, in war there is very little inclination for soldiers to consider an enemy as a feeling human being under any circumstances, and the Japanese made a perfect enemy. They had so many characteristics an American Marine could hate. Physically they were small, a strange color and, by some American standards, unattractive. With the fresh memory of Pearl Harbor in their minds and a few childhood memories of Japanese in bad motion pictures, Marines considered them "sneaky." Further, they did not understand and therefore hated this inscrutable Oriental for his "fanatical" willingness to die. Marines did not consider that they were killing men, their equals. They were wiping out dirty animals burrowed deep in sand under coconut logs, concrete and steel. No matter how they might revise their opinion of the Japanese in later years, this blazing hatred was an effective and necessary stimulant at the time.

Whatever practical or philosophic turn of mind made the Japanese at Tarawa ready to die before being captured, it made the Marines' work difficult. An enemy ready to fight until he is killed is the hardest to beat, and the Japanese killed Marines long after their position was hopeless. Individual Japanese soldiers attached grenades to their belts, pulled the grenade pins and ran screaming towards tanks to throw themselves under the moving treads in the remote hope they would knock out the vehicle and kill the crew. One live Japanese soldier would lie in a pile of dead to fake dead too until the Americans had passed by, then pick up a weapon and fire at them from the rear—so Marines were forced to adopt the unpleasant habit of firing into all the piles of enemy dead to eliminate the chance of one of these fakers.

By late the second day Marine forces had pushed across the narrow island in several places, but the Japanese were far from through. They held dozens of major strongpoints with heavy firepower, and hundreds of smaller pillboxes and gun positions. There were still individual Japanese snipers hanging from the coconut trees that remained standing, and in a few areas there were organized Japanese units—one with as many as five hundred men.

Early in the morning of the third day it became apparent that there were three major Japanese positions near the pier that had to be eliminated. The three positions had mutually covering fire so that it was impossible to attack one at a time. One was a steel pillbox, the second was a coconut-log machine-gun emplacement, and the third was the largest bombproof shelter on the island, situated three hundred yards inland. This bunker was built of concrete wall re-enforced with steel five feet thick, and covered with as much as fifteen feet of sand. Although most of it was below ground, the shelter was of such size that, with its sand cover, the summit was the highest point on the island.

At 9:30 on the third morning a company of mortars scored a direct hit on top of the coconut-log gun position. The ammunition dump next to the position exploded—and this effectively eliminated one of the three strongpoints, enabling the men going for the other two to move up with fire eliminated from that direction at least.

At about the same time, a Sherman tank trundled into position near the steel pillbox and, with its seventy-five booming away, scored a series of direct-line hits. This tends to shake up a man as if he were inside a steel drum, and no more was heard from that position. It is probable the gunners inside were killed by concussion.

The giant bombproof now remained to be taken. Marines had discovered a remarkably effective, if horrible, way of elimi-

Debris provides new hiding places.

Marines work their way to the top of a concealed bomb shelter.

nating these. Each bombproof shelter had a kind of ventilating system which proved to be its Achilles' heel. If Marines could force their way to the top, out of the arc of Japanese fire, they simply poured a drum of gasoline down the Japanese air intake system, then stepped back and threw a grenade into the opening. It was, as a matter of fact, this method that incinerated the Japanese commanding admiral in a bombproof shelter in the afternoon of the second day.

The hot fight for the top of this giant bombproof lasted about an hour. It was a costly fight for the Marines, and as they reached the top a force of about seventy-five Japanese soldiers launched a counterattack to drive them off. King of the mountain was a great Marine, a lean, handsome Princetonian, Lieutenant Alexander Bonnyman. Bonnyman, with his men behind him, stood fast and met the wild countering charge with a flame-thrower grasped in his strong hands. Instead of retreating, Bonnyman moved toward the enemy scrambling up the sandy hillside. Most of them were burned and the rest killed by rifle fire. They were wiped out without achieving anything except the death of one more fine American who had advanced in the face of flying bullets. As the attack died, Bonnyman fell forward and died of his wounds within a few feet of the Japanese he had beaten back.

Now the Japanese inside the huge shelter, aware of the gasoline method, started a frantic scramble to run for safety from two of its four exits. Marines had positioned themselves a short distance from these doors, and mowed the Japanese down with machine-gun fire and an occasional grenade. Engineers blasted the third exit and then, with an unknown number of Japanese still inside, a detachment of Marines was stationed at the fourth exit. Shortly after, one of the war's most underrated pieces of equipment, the common bulldozer, nosed up and effectively sealed off this last way out. It was the final touch to the elimination of these three Japanese strongpoints. The battalion now moved more freely across the island.

The story of Alexander Bonnyman is a Marine legend, but there are probably fifty stories like it which will never be told because the men who saw the action died before they could report it. All across the island Marines were eliminating pillboxes, bunkers and log machine-gun points. Someone always had to go first into direct fire. A group of twenty Marines would charge a pillbox and, because the Japanese could not kill them as fast as they came, some always got close enough to toss a block of TNT or a grenade through a gun hole. In front of every blasted Japanese fortification lay two, three or a dozen fallen Marines. It seemed unfair that, having forced their way ashore, Marines had to continue dying in an operation which by now could only end in victory.

Japanese resistance was not limited to desperate defense from their walled holes. In the afternoon of the third day the first of several Japanese banzai attacks was launched. The Marines' interpretation of the bloodcurdling Japanese yells of *"Banzai!"* was "Nearer my God to Thee." It was, for the Americans, a matter of killing them fast so that they never got close enough to throw their grenades. Frequently the Japanese pulled their grenade pins as they started their wild charge, so that if they were killed close to the Marine lines the blast might still reach a few Americans.

These attacks continued into the night of the third day. During the early evening there were three Japanese counter-attacks by forces of about fifty men. With communications in working order and naval and air support ready and willing to lay down any barrage the infantrymen asked for, most of these attacks were stalled before they got started. Naval gunfire was accurate and Marine artillery that had landed on Bairiki, the small island off the end of Betio, was laying down patterns within seventy-five yards of entrenched Marines without scratching them. Even aircraft strafing, which the foot soldier never trusts to kill more of the enemy than of his friends, was precise.

The most powerful Japanese counterattack was launched at 4 A.M. in the early morning of the fourth and final day of the battle of Tarawa. Two early probing attacks were launched first and it was known the Japanese were searching out Marine strength for a weak spot along the thin line. At about 3 A.M. the enemy started pouring light and heavy machine-gun fire into the Marines from a group of wrecked trucks not more than fifty yards away. Three of these Japanese guns were destroyed by volunteer Marines, who crawled on their bellies in front of their own lines until they were close enough to blast the trucks with grenades. These are Marines who, because their moves were covered by the anonymity of darkness and because bravery here was the normal instead of the unusual, were in all probability never decorated. It is the sort of thing that makes soldiers who fought smile at the rows of medals on the chests of ranking officers. There were brave generals and admirals but their bravery was different; few of them called on themselves to move toward a vicious enemy in pitch-blackness across a battlefield crisscrossed with rifle fire.

When the full-strength banzai attack came at 4 A.M. it was directed against two decimated Marine companies which had crossed the island and were moving down the beach to clean out pillboxes and gun positions on that strongly defended shoreline. Three hundred battle-crazed Japanese charged the outnumbered Marines with bloodcurdling screams of "Marine you die!" or "Japanese drink Marine's blood!"

By radio one of the two company commanders asked battalion headquarters for help:

WE NEED RE-ENFORCEMENTS. THEY ARE COMING AT US FASTER THAN WE CAN KILL THEM.

At battalion headquarters the message shot back:

WE HAVE NO HELP TO SEND. YOU MUST HOLD.

It would have been certain death for the Marines to turn and run. They held. Counterattacking Japanese were held off, the night of terror was ended, and when the sun rose the morning of the fourth day the bodies of two hundred dead Japanese lay strewn in the sand and coral a short distance in front of the Marine company's line.

THE LAST DAY

At eight o'clock on November 23, the fourth day, one infantry battalion supported by two medium tanks, seven light tanks, ample artillery and a company of engineer flame-throwers started towards the small end of the island where the last of the Japanese were still holed up. There were about five hundred enemy left, but things were finally going more the way they had told Marines they would in boot camp. Heavy fire was brought down on the Japanese positions; tanks moved up protecting infantrymen behind them. Naval gunfire was laid down in a continuous barrage at the tip of the island to prevent Japanese from escaping to the neighboring strip of coral, the island of Bairiki. Marines reached the end of the island by three that afternoon. In seven hours they killed 475 Japanese, lost nine of their own and took fourteen prisoners, most of whom were Korean laborers.

General Julian C. Smith, who had come ashore the previous day, sent this message to Admiral Harry Hill on board *Maryland*.

DECISIVE DEFEAT HEAVY ENEMY COUNTERATTACK LAST NIGHT DESTROYED BULK OF HOSTILE RESISTANCE. EXPECT COMPLETE ANNIHILATION OF ENEMY ON BETIO THIS DATE. STRONGLY RECOMMEND THAT YOU AND YOUR CHIEF OF STAFF COME ASHORE THIS DATE TO GET INFORMATION ABOUT TYPE OF HOSTILE RESISTANCE WHICH WILL BE ENCOUNTERED IN FUTURE OPERATIONS.

If Admiral Hill cracked General Smith's code the message read something like this: "Why don't you Navy sons-a-bitches get off your fat tails and come in here to see how the Marines are winning this war?" The Marines, in fact, would have been delighted if all Americans at home could have stood on some square foot of Betio that stinking morning just long enough to make them sick at their stomachs. Having done it, the Marines at Tarawa were frustrated now, knowing the people at home would never understand exactly what it had been like.

The military experts will argue for as long as they talk about

The Japanese who aren't killed by Marines kill themselves by pulling their rifle triggers with their toes.

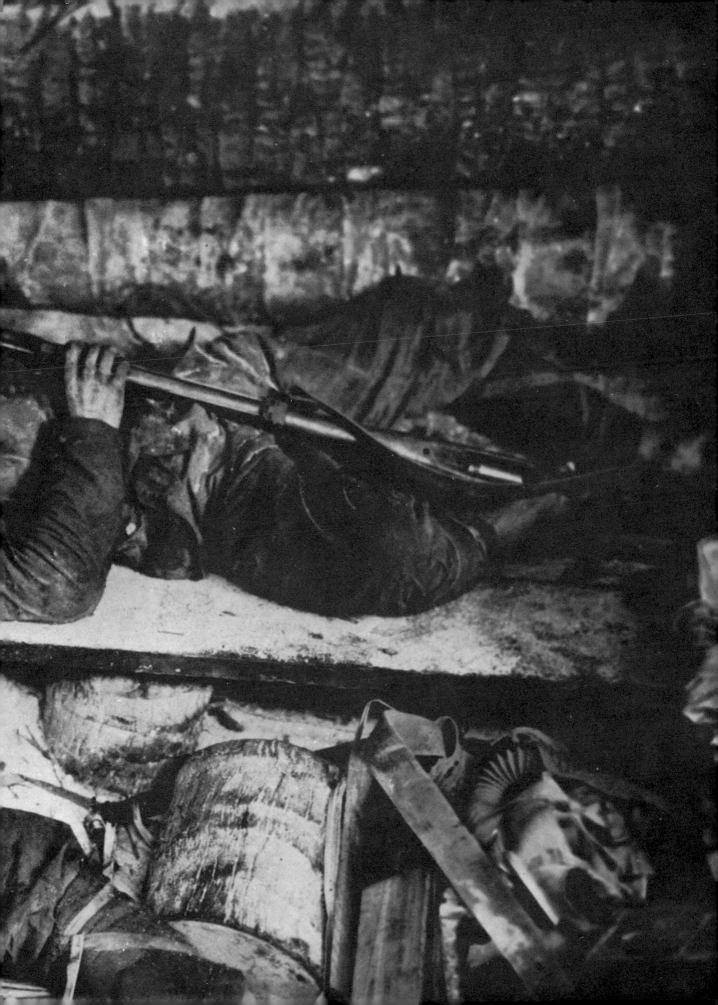

World War II whether one square mile of coral in the Central Pacific was worth the battle. The statistics are these:

JAPANESE CASUALTIES

Total number killed	4690
Prisoners of war taken	17
Escaped	0

AMERICAN CASUALTIES

Total number killed	1026
Total wounded	2296

There were other battles longer, others in which more men died, others of greater importance; but Tarawa was the bitterest, the fiercest, the most concentrated battle of World War II. Tarawa was the very essence of the horrors of war.

STALINGRAD

PICTURE IT 1941. The German Army has successfully landed three million men, ten thousand tanks, 2500 fighting aircraft and millions of tons of ammunition and equipment on the East Coast of the United States. The Germans are driving inland on a broad front from Pennsylvania to Georgia, but their spearhead is aimed at Chicago.

Chicago is Moscow, Memphis is Stalingrad, New Orleans is Astrakhan. The Volga (picture it as America's great river, down which Huck Finn sailed on a raft) runs from way back of Chicago down through Memphis and into the Caspian Sea at New Orleans. It is wide and important.

The Germans are better equipped, better organized; but Americans are defending the country they love. Although not ready for the war, they finally stop the Germans in front of Chicago, on a line running roughly from South Bend to Gary. The Germans are halted by a combination of American determination and winter weather. The winter, even for Chicago, is very severe, and the German supply lines are extended. They suffer huge losses. It is a humiliating and costly defeat but Hitler knows that they are still the stronger force.

As spring approaches, Hitler makes a decision to abandon the attack on Chicago. It is nothing but a symbol of the heart of America, he says. He issues orders for the Wehrmacht to veer sharply south and concentrate on a drive for Memphis. If they can take Memphis and New Orleans, Hitler says they will control the Volga. They will then drive southwest to the rich oilfields of Texas, and west to the wheatfields of the midlands.

With Memphis and New Orleans in his hands, Hitler knows he can cut off the huge quantities of vital Lend-Lease supplies being funneled into the States from the south through the Gulf of Mexico and up the Volga and a network of north–south rail lines.

THERE WERE MANY ELEMENTS of likeness in the geography of the situation in Russia late in 1941. After his conquests of Poland, Czechoslovakia, Norway, Denmark, Belgium and France, Adolf

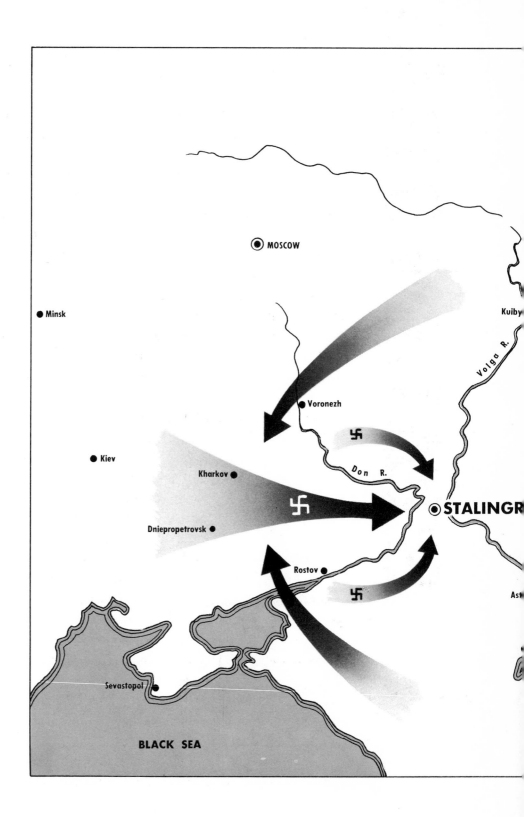

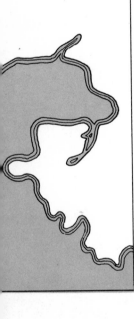

Hitler, the most ambitious man in all history, turned his forces to the east. He threw 70 per cent of his armed might into a titanic battle to conquer the Russians. With 240 infantry and armored divisions of approximately 12,000 men each, the Germans held a line that stretched from near Leningrad, on the Baltic Sea in the north, to a point near Odessa on the Black Sea in the south. Hitler's original goal was Moscow, and his arrogant army of half a million men which had never been defeated had come within twenty-five miles of reaching it.

On December 6, 1941, the Russians launched a counter-offensive under General Georgi Zhukov. In one month the German army lost 100,000 men, 2901 tanks and 1136 planes and Moscow was, for the time being, safe. After continuing losses through the winter and early spring of 1942, Hitler began to understand that he could not take Moscow against the major Russian forces defending it, and a new plan took shape in his mind. He would, instead, order his armies to smash into southern Russia, capture Stalingrad, Rostov, Astrakhan, and continue into the Ukraine and down into the Caucasian oilfields.

Everything to eat in Russia grew in the Ukraine; Caucasian oil ran every Russian vehicle; and Stalingrad, a sort of Red Pittsburgh, not only produced an important share of Russia's heavy machinery but dominated the Volga River, the single most important artery in the Soviet Union. Millions of tons of food, oil, machinery and American Lead-Lease equipment were being carried towards Moscow on its broad waters. Having failed to bring Moscow to its knees with direct military action, Hitler was going to starve out the Russian capital. It was the first of a series of actions that was to bring disaster to the Germans.

(Simultaneously with this superwar in Russia, the Germans were: (*1*) policing half a dozen defeated countries with an iron hand, (*2*) carrying on their war of extermination against several million Jews, (*3*) fighting the British in North Africa, (*4*) bombing England, and (*5*) making a fortress out of the coast of France in anticipation of an Allied invasion.)

The great German summer offensive to the south was scheduled to begin June 28, 1942. Three powerful armies were poised

for the jump-off. They were the predominantly armored Fourth Panzer Army, the Second Army, and Friedrich von Paulus's crack Sixth Army. It was the Sixth which had covered itself with glory in German eyes (and with shame in the eyes of the rest of the world) when it blitzed its way through Belgium, Holland and France.

On June 19, the operations officer of the 23rd Panzer Division, one of the attacking units, was shot down in an observation plane flying over the area between Russian and German lines. When it was learned he had carried with him detailed top-secret plans for the great offensive, German scout troops were sent out. They reached the plane but found no evidence of the operations officer or any of the plans, and it was assumed the Russians had both. The incident sent a wave of panic rippling back up through the chain of command. The German commanders were faced with the question of whether to change every detail of the plan or go through with it. They made the decision to proceed with the attack on schedule and it was evidence of their overpowering strength that, having in effect told the Russians where they were coming and when, they came there and then, and were not stopped.

THE BEGINNING

The early morning of June 28 could be called the beginning of the fateful battle of Stalingrad. The Fourth Panzer and the Second Army, directed by Field Marshal Fedor von Bock, moved out with three armored divisions, three motorized divisions and nine infantry divisions in its forward lines. The southern flanks were being covered by four Hungarian divisions, of whose fighting abilities the Germans were contemptuous. Two German and six additional Hungarian divisions were in reserve. The Sixth Army comprised two armored, one motorized and sixteen infantry divisions.

The Russian steppes, being the opposite of what the word suggests in English, were the perfect battlefield for panzer divisions. Tanks are most effective when they can be maneuvered as an admiral would maneuver ships in a naval battle, and the broad, flat, treeless Russian steppes offered textbook conditions for tank warfare. Under textbook conditions the German soldier has always been invincible; through these midsummer days they swept the Russians in front of them. Air and artillery reduced Russian strongpoints and the tanks surged forward followed by mechanized divisions, infantry in force and finally service troops.

Marshal Timoshenko ordered the Sixty-second Siberian Army, under General Vasili Chuikov, into the battle; and although the Germans continued to smash forward, there were forebodings of what was to come. Winter arrives early in the steppes, and even in late July many Germans who had been trapped in the snow at Moscow could have felt a chill wind in the air and more than one Nazi commander must have cast an apprehensive glance over his epaulets toward the long road home. An army needs staggering daily quantities of food and supplies, and the road over which these supplies had to be hauled was not an unobstructed eight-lane highway. And there were the Partisans. Russian Partisans organized in efficient fighting groups of forty men and often a few women. No bridge along the German supply route could be left unprotected. The Partisans took over the fight wherever the Russian Army had been driven out. Striking like Marion's Men, they came out of hiding at night to bedevil supply lines and rear-echelon units of the Wehrmacht. If the Germans pushed ten thousand men five miles, they had to drop a substantial trail of guards behind to hold what they had passed through. No square mile of Russia was ever really taken as far as the Russians were concerned. The Russian novelist and poet Konstantin Simonov caught the attitude:

IF YOU DON'T WANT TO SURRENDER
TO THE BLACK-HEARTED GERMAN
YOUR HOME, YOUR WIFE, YOUR MOTHER—
EVERYTHING THAT WE CALL THE FATHERLAND—
KNOW THIS: NO ONE SAVES THEM IF YOU DO NOT
SAVE THEM.
KNOW THIS: NO ONE KILLS HIM
IF YOU DO NOT KILL HIM.

For every mile the Germans conquered, their leading elements were diminished by the number who had to be left behind. The Partisans infuriated the Germans.

On July 11, near the town of Beketova, the Germans stationed small parties of guards to direct a supply column of trucks more than nine miles long which was due to pass through the area shortly before midnight. At one of the points where there was a major branch in the road, a party of five German soldiers set up markers and stationed themselves there to make sure the markers were not removed before the column passed. An audacious band of Partisans swooped down on the traffic detail, killing all five. With the help of a few dozen townspeople who risked their lives, they changed the signs and moved a small shed into one of the two roads in a position which obscured the German's correct route. The column of several hundred German supply trucks was led down a road that rapidly deteriorated into a cowpath. The Russian raiders destroyed a small bridge behind the German column after it had passed, and the Partisans spent the next three days sniping at the truck drivers and exploding ammunition-laden trucks caught in a giant traffic tangle.

Although the damage was done and the supply train—what was left of it—reached the front several days late, the Germans retaliated in predictable fashion. In the playground of a small schoolyard on the edge of Beketova, they removed the seats of the swings and threw five lengths of wire over the crossbar. Four Russian men and one woman were stripped of their clothes. They were made to stand on barrels under the swing and one by one, as a wire loop was placed over a head, around a neck, a barrel was rolled out from beneath two kicking feet.

German soldiers had been propagandized to believe that they were invading Russia to forestall an attack on their homeland at some vague date in the future; but there was nothing vague about what the Russians were fighting for. They were fighting for their lives and for their country. There were no rules of war observed.

"The Russians," Hitler said, "are cruel, bestial, animal opponents."

Stalin answered: "The German thieves want a war of extermination with the people of the U.S.S.R. Well, if the Germans want a war of extermination, they will get it."

While the Partisans harried the Germans from the rear, Chuikov's Sixty-second Siberian was conducting an efficient war of attrition against the leading elements of the German Army. At the time, the rest of the world was ill-informed about what was happening, because neither side allowed true reporting. German propaganda reports, leaking to the outside world through neutral countries, didn't have any relation to the facts. They reported only the great German advances with no indication of the losses they were suffering. One cartoon in a United States paper, however, showed Hitler announcing another great victory to the German people, and behind him one of his general staff was whispering to another: "One more victory like this and we'll be wiped out."

Accurate information was equally hard to get from the Russians. American and British reporters in Moscow had to take what information they were given. They themselves were never allowed to go to the front for a look, despite the compelling argument that Americans had a right to know how the Russians were using the staggering quantities of Lend-Lease equipment they had in their possession. Stalin, in effect, told American newsmen and officials, "Go to hell and keep sending the stuff. We'll decide how to use it." And, inasmuch as the Russians were doing most of the fighting and the dying, Americans were in no position to stomp off in a fit of pique and stop the flow of supplies.

So for lack of any impartial reporting it was not clear then and is not clear now to what extent the Russian retreat was by design and to what extent they were forced back. No matter which it was, it proved in the end to be Hitler's undoing. The sharp point of his sword was being constantly dulled and the blade weakened as he shoved it deeper into Russia. The Germans were never stopped, but every day they lost fifty or a hundred tanks

The Russians use every obstacle as a fortress on the steppes.

and the next day the experienced dead were replaced by the inexperienced living. Every mile of advance meant another mile of road behind them to protect. Tenuously held supply lines lengthened. Retreating Russians had a hundred tricks for exacting a high toll from advancing Germans.

For example, they would place the heavier of two available artillery pieces in direct line of a German tank advance, concealing it cleverly in a half-buried position. A second, lighter gun would be concealed in an area flanking the panzer unit to the right or left as it advanced. The heavier gun would remain concealed and on signal the lighter, flanking gun would open fire. German tanks would spin on their tracks left—or right—and open fire on their tormentor. Because the armor is thickest on the front of a tank, this immediately exposed their broader and more vulnerable sides to the heavy Russian fieldpiece. In this way the Red artillerymen often could destroy six or eight German tanks in a single engagement, before they hurriedly picked up and ran.

STALINGRAD FALLS—ALMOST

Yet despite everything the Russians were doing to delay the advance, the Sixth Army and the Fourth Panzer Army swept relentlessly east toward the Don River. The Don curves in a wide-mouthed, irregular U near Stalingrad, its closest point being about forty miles away. Stalingrad itself is on the west banks of the Volga, which turns easterly, north and south of the city. The Don was the last natural barrier between the Germans and this double prize, Stalingrad and the Volga. By the middle of July, Hitler was convinced that the Russian Army had collapsed; and he was so contemptuous of the timidity of his own General Staff that he established a personal command headquarters in a small triangle of woods near Vinnitsa, a Ukranian town two hundred and fifty miles from the Czech border.

Confident now that the Sixth Army could take the city alone, and further aware that he must capture the Caucasian oilfields around Baku by October if his armored columns were not going to face another winter without sufficient fuel, as they had at Moscow, Hitler ordered the Fourth Panzer Army supporting the Sixth to wheel south toward Rostov. It was this order, issued from his Ukrainian command position, which postwar German military writers invariably refer to as "the single most tragic error in the battle for Stalingrad." "Tragic" in German eyes, but to the rest of the world it must remain a most thoroughly happy error, because it led directly to the annihilation of the Sixth Army.

While the First and Fourth Panzer Armies were making short work of Rostov, the Sixth, without armored help, ground to a halt on the Don River line. With Rostov in German hands, Hitler ordered the weary Fourth Panzer to turn once more and approach Stalingrad from the south, assuming that pressure from that direction would allow the Sixth to move again. The damage had been done, however. Rostov was three hundred miles from the nearest Sixth Army elements. It took about two gallons of gas to move one tank one mile, and the Fourth Panzer had consumed huge quantities of scarce fuel and two weeks of precious time. The Russians had used that time to turn the city of Stalingrad into a fortress. They had moved in large numbers of reenforcements, and had formed a tight semicircle on the east banks of two small streams about eighteen miles in front of Stalingrad. Neither did they completely abandon their positions across the Don from the Germans. Since the German offensive began on June 28, the Russians had lost a staggering total of a quarter of a million men. Roads were clogged with burned-out equipment and Russian dead; but the Russians were far from beaten. Into that forty-mile strip of land between the Don and the Volga were compressed all the units which had survived the retreat, and the re-enforcements which had been pumped in.

In Moscow Joseph Stalin reorganized his high command and replaced Marshal Timoshenko with Georgi Zhukov as leader of the forces defending all of southern Russia. Stalin created a new Supreme Army command and to no one's surprise named himself as overall boss. Timoshenko as northern leader worked directly under Stalin till October 1942. Thus the stage was set for this

epic struggle between two great armies led by the two most powerful dictators the world had ever known. It was apparent from Hitler's actions in taking up a command position on Russian soil, and in superimposing his will on the better military judgment of his experienced generals, that he saw in Stalingrad more than a strategically placed industrial city. The very name infuriated him! Stalin's City. It was a symbol of everything he wanted to crush under his heel.

At ten minutes past three on the morning of August 21, the Germans started their push to cross the Don. More than one hundred assault boats, each carrying about fifty men, started shuttling back and forth across the river. In the narrower parts specially designed cork rafts were used and by morning six Wehrmacht infantry regiments had established a bridgehead across the water barrier that had stalled the German advance for twelve days. Resistance came mostly from Russian machine-gunners, and, for a war that didn't consider a few thousand men as many, losses were light.

By 4:30 on the afternoon of August 23, engineers had thrown up two twenty-ton pontoon bridges, and the German troops which had been contained in the big bend on the west side of the Don started pouring across. Ahead of them lay thirty-six miles of open steppe country with an occasional small stream, a few villages and, to the north of Stalingrad, the main rail line towards Moscow. With plenty of air support from dive-bombing Stukas, German infantrymen in trucks and rumbling armored columns churned towards Stalingrad on the Volga. Occasionally a small artillery piece would open fire on the German columns or machine-gun and rifle fire would erupt from a farmhouse. Wehrmacht soldiers were drained from their trucks, there was a brief fire-fight, and then with the pocket of resistance eliminated the column moved quickly forward.

Always the effort to salvage the prized possession.

When it became apparent that the Germans were going to reach Stalingrad, Soviet authorities there started a mass effort to remove as much of the machinery as possible from the invaluable war-production plants of the city. This brought a telephone call from Joseph Stalin in Moscow: "Stop this evacuation. Stalingrad must be held at any price. Soldiers will fight harder for a live city than for an empty one." He ordered every Russian soldier to fight to the end.

Hitler boomed back with his own oratorical artillery: "The occupation of Stalingrad, which will be concluded, will deepen and strengthen our success . . . and you can be certain that no human being will ever push us away from that spot."

On August 26 the Luftwaffe subjected Stalingrad to what, at that point in the war, was the most devastating air attack ever made, while on the ground German tanks were supported for the first time with rocket-firing artillery. They were losing five hundred men a day, but they were inching relentlessly towards the outskirts of the city. Hitler was like a race horse wearing blinders. He could see nothing except what was straight ahead—Stalingrad. His Chief of Staff, General Franz Halder, warned him repeatedly that this German thrust into Russia was dangerously exposed on both its northern and southern flanks. When Halder presented Hitler with Intelligence statistics which showed that Timoshenko was sending troops down from the Moscow defense line and concentrating them north of Stalingrad, the self-appointed German military expert flew into a rage, screaming at the monocled Prussian officer: "Don't tell me this idiotic nonsense!"

Stalingrad—which has been renamed Volgograd—stretches for more than twenty miles along the mile-wide Volga River and, as with any city of 700,000, its outskirts meld with peripheral villages. Its boundaries are not always apparent, and for this reason it is difficult to pinpoint the date on which German forces entered its city limits. It was about September 1. One spearhead of the 79th Panzer Grenadier Regiment reached the Volga north of Stalingrad and an armored engineer battalion crossed the four-track railway lifeline running into

Stalingrad, cutting off any further Russian hopes for supplies, except through the rear door, across the Volga. At the same time these panzer units captured two Russian ferryboats. The fact that each of these river ships was capable of carrying twenty-seven railroad cars is an indication of the extent to which the Volga was used for transportation.

During the first ten days of September, German armored and infantry prongs pushed into Stalingrad from a dozen angles. The half-million civilians were either compressed into Russian-held sections of the city or overrun and ordered to march west by the Germans. With the city's back to the river, there was no place for them to run. There was no transportation for them across the Volga, because everything that would float was being used to move equipment and supplies for the besieged Russian Army. Those civilians oozed out westward in long, dreary columns. Uncounted thousands of them died, because there was nothing west as far as the Czech border but the desolate battlefields of the past months. These people were without food, and the land had been stripped of everything of any possible use to a human being. The German Army would not, and as a matter of fact could not, feed them; so they walked, headed nowhere, until they dropped of starvation or died at night of exposure.

On September 8 about three hundred and fifty Russian tanks, many of them American Lend-Lease Sherman M-4s, attacked the Germans to the north, but almost half the tanks were destroyed and the attack was a failure. On September 14 a German panzer column reached the heart of Stalingrad and took the highest point in town, an ancient cemetery area known as the "Mamai Kurgan." This site dominated all of Stalingrad; with this position in their hands the Germans had an observation post from which they could direct dive-bombing Stukas and artillery fire.

The Russians realized this would make Stalingrad almost impossible for them to hold. General Alexander Rodimstev, commanding the 13th Guards Rifles, a first-rate Russian division, had been attacking German positions from the rear by coming down on them from the north, along the west side of the Volga. When the Mamai Kurgan fell into German hands, this division was

given the job of taking it back. In a huge ferrying operation, the division crossed to the east side of the Volga, marched down to a point opposite the center of Stalingrad and once more crossed the river. From the river-edge landing position they moved to the center of town, and, in a battle reminiscent of Bunker Hill, stormed this metropolitan mountain. Seven thousand Russians died in the charge; but by September 16 the Germans were driven from the Mamai Kurgan.

THE FIGHT IN THE STREETS

With two men rolling over in a back-alley brawl it is difficult to tell which is holding the other or who has the best of it. It was this way in Stalingrad for much of September and October. The Germans, by late September, had cut off the city from three sides and the only Russian entry was from across the river behind it. But the Germans were losing men and equipment in large numbers every day, and for them one German tank or one soldier or one slice of bread was harder to resupply than two tanks, ten men or a loaf of bread for the Russians.

The battle became a dogfight in the streets of Stalingrad. The Germans, who had so purposefully reduced many of the city's houses, factories, and public buildings to ruins, found that while they had destroyed a city they had built a devil's fortress for the defenders. Every shellhole in the street, every shattered house, each crack in a wall was used as a hard point of resistance. Every building and every heap of rubble on every street was fought for. When the Germans tried to move into a large building partially intact and occupied by Russians they had to fight not for the building but for each room in the building. Forced off one floor, the defenders would move up a flight or into the cellar and fight for that. Small battles raged down the halls of large municipal buildings. A desk or a broom closet was the private fortress of one or two soldiers. One large building was occupied by Germans, who established a radio center in its basement. Russians, with their greater familiarity with their own city, located nearby a still-intact water main; from there they covered the basement exits with small artillery pieces, to contain the Germans; then they burst the water main, drowning the trapped Germans as the basement water rose to the ceiling.

This was not the Germans' kind of war. There was no grand plan, no masterly movement of men, and their tanks were useless except on the outer fringes of the city. On November 3, this message was sent over one of the hundred-watt transmitters in von Paulus's headquarters:

> WE CANNOT TAKE COMPLETE POSSESSION OF THE CITY WITH PRESENT FORCES DUE TO HIGH RATE OF CASUALTIES. REQUEST ASSAULT GROUPS AND STREET-FIGHTING SPECIALISTS.

In every war the best street-fighters have been men fighting in their own streets against an invader. Stalin's order to stop the evacuation of civilian workers and factory equipment had the effect of making Stalingrad a living city for its defenders. It was not an empty ghost town; the factories under siege were actually still producing tractors, trucks and submachine guns. During the month of September, in spite of dive-bomber attacks and heavy artillery shelling, the Stalingrad Tractor Plant not only repaired tanks but produced two hundred new ones along with one hundred and fifty armored cars.

The siege of Stalingrad, that period during which the Germans were trying to wrest control of the actual city area from the Russians, lasted sixty-six days. The fact that Stalingrad stretched out long and thin along the Volga made it more difficult. The river side of the city sat on bluffs high above the Volga. The bluffs on the east side, fortunately for the Red Army, dominated those on the west banks. General Chuikov's headquarters and his artillery and observation posts were on or behind those eastern river palisades. The bluffs on both sides were honeycombed with rooms and passageways. The Russian civilians who had not been overrun were forced, like victims walking the plank on a pirate ship, to the outermost edge of the western heights. Three important factories were along the river: farthest north was the Stalingrad Tractor Plant, then the Barricades Machine Construction Factory, and, near the center of Stalingrad, the Red October

Metallurgical Plant. These three factories, the heights called the Mamai Kurgan, the river bluffs and the business center were the six principle military objectives. The Germans retook part of the Mamai Kurgan in November; they also captured the Red October Plant and occupied most of the central business district. They now held a funnel-shaped area around Stalingrad.

For the German General Staff, and especially for General Halder, its Chief of Staff, this period was a nightmare during which he kept tapping Hitler on the shoulder but could not call his attention to the gathering storm in the north. Halder knew the German forces were overextended; he knew the Russians were massing large forces north, between Moscow and Stalingrad, as well as south behind the Volga. In a rage, Hitler finally turned on Halder and screamed: "You and I have been suffering from a war of nerves. Half of my nervous exhaustion is due to you. I need National Socialist enthusiasm now, not professional advice, to settle matters in Russia. I cannot expect this of you." With this, Halder was dismissed and Hitler called General Kurt Zeitzler to his headquarters at Vinnitsa.

The postwar tendency to refer to Hitler as a "military idiot" ignores the fact that he almost conquered the world with his audacity. Many of the professional military men on his own General Staff who opposed him most nevertheless recognized the man's mad genius. He had a chessplayer's memory for position, and a special knack for projecting his plans into the future with wild imagination. Added to these talents was his ability to infuse his subordinates with his own enthusiasm for a project.

Hitler was now commuting between Berlin and Vinnitsa several times a week. He would spent a few hours or a day in Berlin handling the details of his war on other fronts, and then return to his primary interest, Stalingrad. On November 9, he made one of his raving speeches in the Burgerbrau Beer Hall before a select group of old-guard Nazis.

The Russians advance even during retreat.

"I wanted to reach the Volga and arrive there at a definite place, a definite city," he shouted. "That city happens to bear the name of Stalin himself. I wanted to take the place and do you know, we have captured it. Except for a few small places, it is in our hands. People ask 'Why does not the Army advance faster?' My answer is that . . . I prefer to reach my objectives by means of limited attacks. Time is not important."

Adolf Hitler must have known that at that very minute time had never been more important to an army. The men, in addition to their other miseries, were now cold both night and day. The Russians on their side were having problems, because ice floes were coming down the river from the frozen north, making navigation across the still unfrozen southern portions of the Volga difficult, and this was their only way of supporting the troops in the city. The Russians desperately wanted a real freeze. They knew they were better equipped than the Germans for cold weather, and when the Volga froze solid it would provide them with a highway instead of a river.

While Hitler's divisions were literally and figuratively bleeding to death, the Russian forces in the north grew stronger. The Germans were taking Stalingrad inch by inch at terrible cost to themselves. In the late afternoon of November 8, after his casualty reports were in, General von Wietersheim, commander of the XIV Panzer Corps, sent this message to von Paulus:

IF THE PRESENT SITUATION CONTINUES, I CAN TELL YOU THE EXACT DAY ON WHICH I WILL LOSE MY LAST MAN.

Von Paulus, the six-foot-six-inch old-style German militarist, immediately sent back a radio message to von Wietersheim:

ARE YOU COMMANDING THE SIXTH ARMY, WIETERSHEIM, OR AM I?

The answer, of course, was that neither of them was. Adolf Hitler was commanding the ill-fated Sixth and von Paulus was his representative on the scene.

On November 9 the Germans started their last great effort to win all of Stalingrad. A regiment of specially trained street-fighting engineers were flown into the three airfields in German hands and these troops were moved into the center of the city for an assault through the ruins on the Russian strongpoints on the river. These positions were on the bluffs one hundred to two hundred feet above the Volga, and the Red docking areas for supplies coming in from the east side of the mile-wide river were directly below them. The drop was so sheer that no mortar or artillery could throw a shell with enough trajectory to hit the docks. The Russians were dug into caverns on the back side of the palisades. They were supported by artillery fire from across the river and from Red gun positions on islands in the river.

Regimental headquarters for the fresh German assault forces were set up in what was left of a block-long factory building. The new officers and troops moved in to make ready for the attack, but before they had established their communications system, eighteen headquarters men were killed by mines and traps the Russians had set as they pulled out of the building. The German move-out was set for sometime around 11 P.M. Shortly before nine o'clock the sounds of a brisk fire-fight broke out in what the Germans thought was secured ground behind them in the business center of Stalingrad. The extensive sewage system for the city flowed into two large underground waterways that emptied into the Volga near the Russian positions on the river, and a detachment of about fifty Russian soldiers, armed with submachine guns, had made their way through it to a point behind the German front lines. Rising out of manholes over an area of several blocks, these Russian infantrymen further disrupted the newly placed and bewildered German assault regiment.

The German offensive designed to split the Russian forces holding the twenty-mile river bluff started on schedule, despite the harassing actions of the Russian "underground." The Germans felt that if they could gain one position along the cliff, above the river, they could disrupt Russian supply boats plying between the east and west banks.

With typical thoroughness, the Germans had labeled or numbered every pile of rubble, every half-standing building, and

assigned a unit to take it. Despite their continued superiority in numbers and equipment, their losses were heavy and each defended position took hours to reduce. Hung in a museum as an oil painting, any one of the piles might appropriately have been labeled "Horror." Bricks, legs, wood beams, arms, steel, pieces of human heads, broken rifles and clothing were mingled as if someone had made an unsuccessful attempt to homogenize these elements. When the Germans found some piece of a building standing with even a part of a room that offered some protection, they would often lie down, side by side with the dead Russians, to catch an hour's sleep. Frequently two or three Red soldiers who had been buried alive but had escaped death would work their way to the surface like ants out of a hill that has been stepped on and open fire on a German unit that thought it was safe from the rear at least. On the night of November 12, three Russians crept to the first floor of a sturdy brick building, part of which remained standing, and bayoneted a German colonel and two radio operators who were using a small bathroom as a command post from which to direct the attack. Germans still occupying the room above bored holes in the concrete floor and poured liquid flame down on the marauding Reds.

This scramble through the ruins of Stalingrad, which continued through November 19, was called the *Rattenkreig* ("Rat War") by the Germans. It was a dirty fight in every sense, with all the hate of the long campaign behind them coming out as these two forces met in rubble alleys. The Russians did not waste a bullet if they could knife or bayonet a German through the throat; and the Germans, so fearful of the Russians' trick of popping up to their rear, put bullets into every Russian they found, dead or alive.

There were no prisoners now, no burial parties. Such niceties of war as caring for the overrun wounded of the enemy were dispensed with in favor of a bullet through the head.

By November 14, the last German push had expended all its energy, manpower and ammunition. It had, in actual fact, reached not one but two high points over the Volga River, but in such small force as to be meaningless. To be effective, a German position on the river needed artillery and soldiers in division numbers. Here it was as if a weary band of mountain climbers had reached the peak of Mt. Everest with their last ounce of strength.

This pin-point probe to the edge of the Volga was as close as Adolf Hitler came to conquering Russia. For five days both sides hung on to what they had; then on that fateful day—November 19, 1942—the Russians sprung their trap.

THE PINCERS

At a few minutes past midnight, November 19, the German meteorologist attached to Sixth Army Headquarters jotted three brief notes in a large, black leatherbound book he kept. Translated, they read: *"Temperature:* 18 degrees. *Precipitation:* Snow. *Wind:* 41 miles per hour."

At exactly 4 A.M. there was a rumble that sounded like thunder seventy-five miles northeast of Stalingrad. Eight hundred Russian artillery pieces started a rain of steel and fire on the Third Romanian Army protecting the northeastern German flank. The fire was concentrated on one two-mile-long area of the Romanian line and it was devastating. Pillboxes, dug-in gun positions and trenches were blasted open. The weather and the Russians hit the Germans at Stalingrad at precisely the same time.

At 8 A.M. the Russian tanks started rolling out of their hidden positions in the Kremenskaya forest. They came fifty abreast across the rolling steppes, and they came relentlessly under the haze of smoke and fire, bearing down on such Romanian troops as had not already turned and fled.

The long thin Nazi column running into Red Russia was thick where it had piled up against Chuikov's tough Sixty-second Siberians backed against the rock cliffs over the Volga at Stalingrad. Here the Sixth Army now occupied a semicircle about twenty miles long and twelve miles deep. Behind that the long thin supply tube running from the Russian border into Stalingrad was very narrow, and the Germans had entrusted its flank protection to the Second German Army, the Second Hungarian, the Eighth Italian and the Third Romanian. The Germans kept the

Romanian and Hungarian Armies separated like two bad boys, because they were afraid they'd fight between themselves. Elements of the German Second were used with all three of the allied divisions to make sure the sometimes reluctant allies didn't desert the front in large numbers for lack of interest in fighting Hitler's war on the Russian steppes hundreds of miles from their homelands.

Nothing could have stopped that Red avalanche of steel, least of all this relatively weak Romanian Army, whose heaviest weapon was the horse-drawn 37 mm anti-tank gun. Wave after wave of Russian and Russian-manned American tanks surged forward through the two-mile gap blasted by the Red artillery. Every tank was covered with Russian infantrymen like ants on a lump of sugar. Their pockets bulged with grenades, their shoulders were heavy with ribbons of ammunition, and in their hands they clutched the simple, cheap but marvelously effective little Russian submachine gun. The Romanian Army was torn to shreds. What there was left folded back like an opening door, and the Russians poured through.

Meanwhile, south of Stalingrad the Russians had held tenaciously to one small bridgehead on the west bank of the Volga. Now this position served as the base for the other claw of Zhukov's huge pincers. Supplies, tanks, trucks, and infantrymen were moved across the frozen Volga from the east in large numbers, and simultaneously with the attack on the Romanians, to the north, this Russian force attacked rear elements of the German Fourth Panzer Army occupied at Stalingrad.

As more Russian troops were moved down from the Moscow area to attack from the north, and as the Russians built up their forces to the south on the west side of the Volga, their attack gained strength. In addition to infantry and tank divisions, the Russians used two corps of Cossack cavalry to great advantage. Each corps was composed of three or four divisions, and while the size of Russian divisions varied considerably, there were probably fifty thousand saber-swinging horsemen. The Germans belittled the fighting qualities of the Romanian troops, but an inadequately armed man could hardly be called cowardly if, after

a four-hour artillery barrage, he quailed in the face of a charge of several thousand screaming cavalrymen thundering towards his position with sabers drawn.

The Russians believed in using cavalry alone, not mixed with infantry or motorized troops, and they believed in using it in overwhelming strength. Although this may have been history's last great cavalry charge, one was never used with greater effectiveness. The Cossack was completely at home on the steppes astride his horse in snow and cold. He wore high black boots, a caracul cap and a long flowing cloak. A combination hood and scarf was thrown over his shoulders, and in the winter all this was covered with a heavy, black felt burka which came to the ankles. The burka was the Cossack's overcoat, raincoat, and, at night, his blanket; and yet all these layers of clothes that made him comfortable in the piercing cold were so arranged as to leave free his saber-swinging right arm.

For more than twenty-four hours the forces inside Stalingrad itself did not fully realize what was happening. Their own battle seemed of paramount importance. Few soldiers at war know or care what is happening to the left or right of them and they are only vaguely concerned about what is going on to their rear. No other action seems important until it affects them directly.

Sometime during the late afternoon of November 22, the Red Third Guards Mechanized Corps driving down from the north met the Fifth Guards Mechanized Corps pushing up from the south. They joined at Marinovka, just east of the Don River, at a point forty miles directly in front of Stalingrad. The trap had slammed shut on the 270,000 men of von Paulus's Sixth Army.

When Hitler learned of the encirclement, he was wild with anger. He settled first on Lieutenant General Heim, commander of the XLVIII Panzer Corps, one of the German units which had been assigned to give starch to the flimsy Romanian defense. Heim was stripped of his decorations and thrown into the Army prison at Moabit; but, of all the experts at Hitler's headquarters, Hitler alone felt that Heim's battle errors—if indeed he had made any at all—were of any consequence. The Fuehrer's headquarters was torn with dissension, and Hitler thought his whole General Staff was plotting against him. In actual fact, a few had begun to. (It is interesting to note, though, that the German General Staff was brought to the point of rebellion not because of any concern over what Hitler was trying to accomplish in the world but rather because of what it thought were the errors of military tactics with which he was trying to accomplish it.)

Ringed by the Red Army, von Paulus, who had occupied a headquarters building about nine miles from the center of Stalingrad, was forced to pick up and move into the heart of the city. The evacuation was hasty, but before he pulled out von Paulus dispatched this message to General Zeitzler, Hitler's new Chief of Staff:

> ARMY ENCIRCLED. DESPITE HEROIC RESISTANCE, WHOLE OF STALINGRAD VALLEY NOW IN RUSSIAN HANDS. STRONG ENEMY FORCES APPROACHING FROM SOUTHEAST AND IN GREAT STRENGTH FROM NORTHWEST. DON FROZEN, IMPROVING RUSSIAN SUPPLY POSITION. SIXTH ARMY FUEL SUPPLIES ALMOST EXHAUSTED. AMMUNITION SITUATION ACUTE. FOOD SUPPLIES AVAILABLE FOR SIX DAYS ONLY. REQUEST FREEDOM OF DECISION IN THE EVENT OF FAILURE TO RECONSTRUCT DEFENSIVE POSITION. SITUATION COULD COMPEL ABANDONMENT OF STALINGRAD.

Von Paulus had been in communication with Colonel General Freiherr von Weichs, Commander in Chief of Army Group B, which included the Sixth Army and the units behind it. On the same day, von Weichs sent a message to Vinnitsa emphasizing von Paulus's plaintive request:

> DESPITE THE EXCEPTIONAL GRAVITY OF THE DECISION TO BE TAKEN, WITH THE FAR-REACHING CONSEQUENCES OF WHICH I AM WELL AWARE, I MUST REGARD IT AS NECESSARY TO ACCEPT PAULUS'S PROPOSAL FOR THE WITHDRAWAL OF THE SIXTH ARMY. MY REASONS ARE AS FOLLOWS:
>
> (1) THE SUPPLY OF THE TWENTY DIVISIONS WHICH CONSTITUTE THIS ARMY IS NOT FEASIBLE BY AIR. WITH THE AIR

TRANSPORT AVAILABLE AND IN FAVORABLE WEATHER, IT WILL BE POSSIBLE TO SUPPLY THE ENCIRCLED FORCES WITH ONLY ONE TENTH OF THEIR DAILY REQUIREMENTS.

(2) IN VIEW OF THE TIME REQUIRED TO ASSEMBLE A RE-LIEVING FORCE, THE ENCIRCLED TROOPS COULD NOT BE RE-LIEVED WITH A PENETRATION FROM THE OUTSIDE BEFORE DECEMBER 10. THE RAPID DETERIORATION OF THE SIXTH ARMY'S SUPPLIES INDICATES THAT THESE MUST BE EXHAUSTED WITHIN A FEW DAYS. AMMUNITION WILL SOON BE EXPENDED, SINCE THE ENCIRCLED FORCE IS BEING ATTACKED CONTINUALLY FROM ALL SIDES.

I BELIEVE A BREAKTHROUGH BY THE SIXTH ARMY IN A SOUTHWESTERLY DIRECTION WILL RESULT FAVORABLY TO THE SITUATION AS A WHOLE. WITH THE TOTAL DISSOLUTION OF THE ROMANIAN ARMY, THE SIXTH ARMY IS NOW THE ONLY FIGHT-ING UNIT IN THE IMMEDIATE AREA CAPABLE OF INFLICTING DAMAGE ON THE ENEMY.

I AM WELL AWARE THAT THIS PROPOSED OPERATION WILL ENTAIL HEAVY LOSSES, PARTICULARLY IN ARMS AND EQUIP-MENT, BUT THESE WILL BE FAR LESS THAN THOSE THAT MUST FOLLOW IF THE SITUATION IS LEFT TO DEVELOP AS IT IS, WITH THE INEVITABLE STARVING-OUT OF THE ENCIRCLED ARMY AS A RESULT.

FREIHERR VON WEICHS
Colonel General, Army Group B

When von Paulus reached his new headquarters, in what had been the business district of Stalingrad, a message which had come down through the chain of command awaited him. It must have chilled von Paulus more than the cold winds sweeping in off the steppes:

SIXTH ARMY IS TEMPORARILY ENCIRCLED BY RUSSIAN FORCE. IT IS MY INTENTION TO CONCENTRATE SIXTH ARMY IN THE STALINGRAD AREA. SIXTH ARMY MUST BE LEFT IN NO DOUBT THAT I SHALL DO EVERYTHING IN MY POWER TO ENSURE THAT IT RECEIVES SUPPLIES AND THAT IT WILL BE RELIEVED

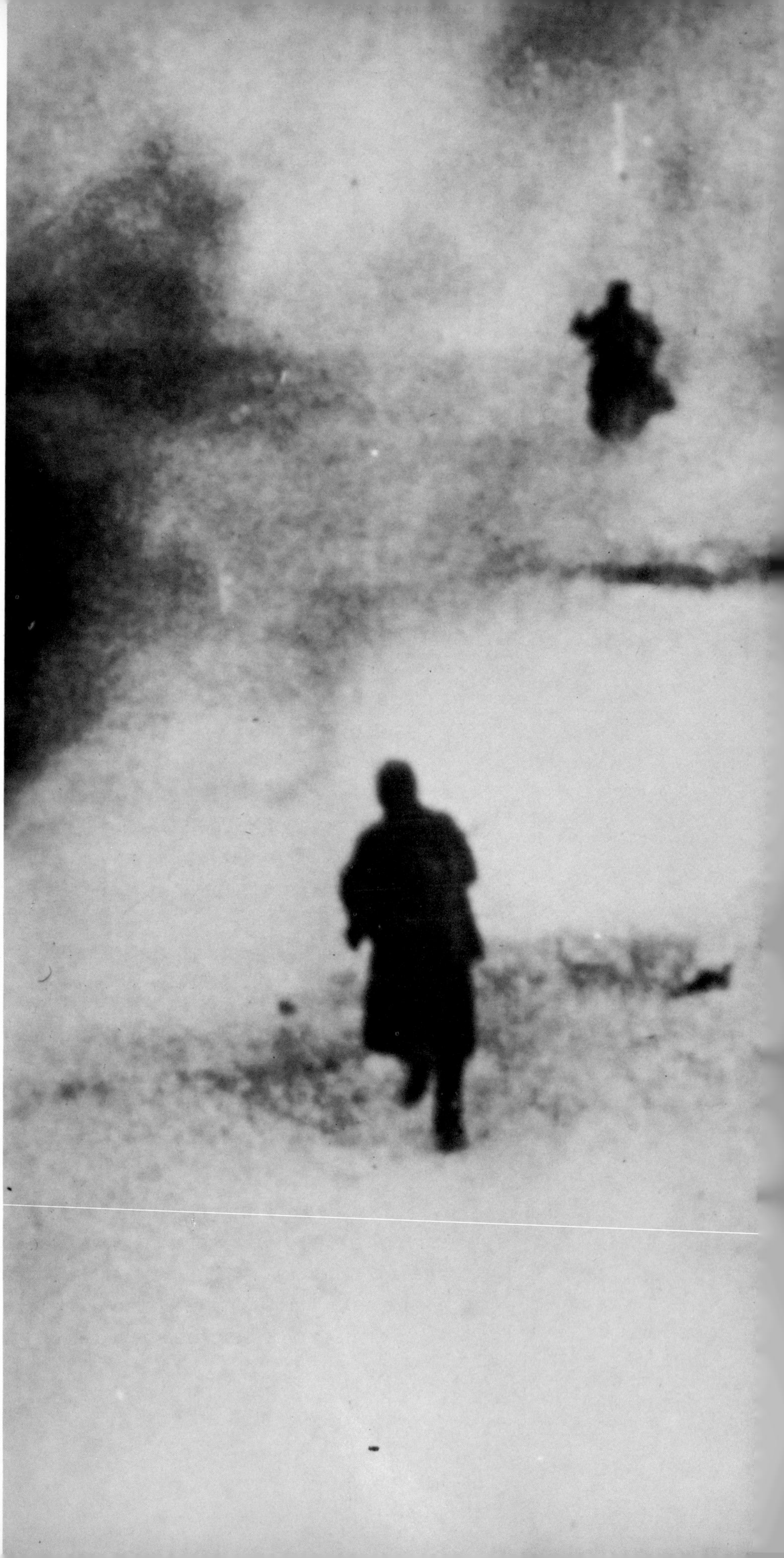

IN DUE COURSE. I KNOW THE BRAVE MEN OF THE SIXTH ARMY AND ITS COMMANDER IN CHIEF, AND I KNOW THAT IT WILL DO ITS DUTY. THOSE UNITS OF THE SIXTH ARMY THAT REMAIN BETWEEN THE DON AND THE VOLGA WILL HENCEFORTH BE DESIGNATED "FORTRESS STALINGRAD."

ADOLF HITLER

Inside Stalingrad the trapped German soldiers were not thinking of master plans and the strategy of moving armies. Each of them was concerned with the life of one man. Letters, most of them never delivered, were written to loved ones at home. The bravest wrote letters of hope, not because they had much, but to spare someone at home the despair they felt. Many wrote sweet letters of sad farewell, and a few wrote letters bitterly critical of those responsible for their plight. But they all wrote.

DEAREST MARTA:

I spoke with Herman today. He is lying a couple of hundred meters from me; we were in the southern part of the front. Not much is left of the regiment, but the son of Brausch, the baker, is still with us. Herman has received the letter in which you told us about the death of Mother and Father. I have tried to comfort him, for I am older, but I too am about at the end of my rope. It is good that Father and Mother will never know that the two of us, Herman and I, are never coming home. It is frightfully cruel that in your future life you must bear the burden of four dead people.

I wanted to become a priest, and Father wanted to have a house where Herman could build a fountain. None of that has happened. You know how it looks at home, and we know quite well how it looks here. No, none of these things that we have envisioned in our plans have come to pass. Our parents lie beneath the wreckage of their house and we, difficult as this may sound, are lying with a couple of hundred others in a ravine. Soon this ravine will be filled with snow. . . .

Love,

GERHARDT

The letters were written by the educated and the uneducated. Most of them went undelivered by Hitler's orders but a few thousand that were not burned unopened were salvaged by Army correspondents and historians. Some of them speak more effectively for the German soldier as a feeling human being than a thousand postwar apologists. How many were there like this?

. . . These last few nights I have cried so much that it seems unbearable to me. I saw a comrade cry too, but for another reason. He cried for his lost tank, which had been his great pride. It is as incomprehensible to me as my own weakness is, that a man can grieve for dead war material. I have always bowed easily to tears. An upsetting or a noble deed makes me cry. It was that way at the theater or when I read a sad book or saw an animal suffer. . . . I could not cry over tanks. My tears flow in the night.

On Tuesday I destroyed two Russian tanks with the gun on my truck. It was a magnificent and impressive sight. Afterwards, I went past the smoking wreckage. A body hung out of the hatch, head downwards. Its feet were caught fast and on fire to the knees. The body was still alive, its mouth moaning. It must have been horrible pain, and there was no possibility of freeing it. Even if this had been possible the man would have died agonizingly in a few hours. I shot him, and with that tears ran down my cheeks. I have now cried for three nights over the dead Russian tank driver, whose murderer I am. . . . I fear that I shall never be able to sleep peacefully again if I should come home to you. My life is a terrible conflict. . . . Through the night I cry in vain. What will happen now?

The Russian journalist, Ilya Ehrenburg, spoke for many Russians who had wondered whether all Germans could be bad: "Of course, there are in this Army a few thinking and feeling individuals, they are alone among millions; they are ladybirds sitting on the back of a mad elephant. We have neither the time nor the

The once proud.

desire to bother about ladybirds. We must shoot the mad elephant."

In the first few days after the encirclement, German commanders inside and outside the Stalingrad ring knew that the Russian forces surrounding them were thin. They knew too that if they were to burst free the Sixth had to pick up, leave Stalingrad and attack west with all possible strength before the Russian band was re-enforced in an attempt to meet a second German force that would drive east. Zeitzler and the whole German General Staff exerted as much pressure on Hitler as they dared, trying to convince him that he must allow von Paulus to abandon Stalingrad and the Volga. Hitler insisted he would save the Sixth by sending help through from outside.

"It is a crime," Zeitzler said, "to leave the Sixth Army where it is. The entire army must be slaughtered and starved."

At about 2 A.M. on the morning of November 24, a meeting broke up in Hitler's private office at Vinnitsa. It had lasted more than five hours. Hitler—though not convinced—had reluctantly agreed, in the face of overwhelming General Staff opinion, to allow von Paulus to attempt the breakout. The weary generals— no one but the secretary sat at these meetings—dragged out of the Fuehrer's office trying to conceal their satisfaction over having won their point, lest their unpredictable Leader should change his mind. They did not know Hitler had one more appointment before retiring.

Zeitzler surreptitiously informed von Weichs and von Paulus, through one overlooked telephone line, that they would receive their official orders to break out between 7 and 8 A.M.

Through the early morning hours, von Paulus, tall, impeccably monocled, with a twitching left eye that betrayed his apparent implacability, paced across the broken stones of his basement headquarters, waiting for those few words to come sputtering across the teletype machine that might save an army.

At this same time, one more visitor was ushered into Adolf Hitler's office three hundred miles west. It was Hermann Goering, the corpulent Luftwaffe chief, whose ambitions were as boundless as Hitler's own. In a few minutes Goering told Hitler what he wanted to hear. The Luftwaffe, he promised, could supply the trapped Sixth Army with five hundred tons of food, clothing and ammunition a day if von Paulus could maintain control of the three airfields within his compound—Gumrak, Pitomnik and the smaller Stalingradski airfield.

By ten o'clock that morning von Paulus still had no word. Perhaps another general would have taken it upon himself to send out a get-ready order to the commanders under him, but von Paulus's ultimate devotion was to discipline. He waited. The bitter truth came to him late in the day, and it came indirectly through a radio message. Hitler had changed his mind. Goering had given him the support he needed, and on the spot Hitler had made a new decision. He ordered all the rag-tag units outside the Stalingrad ring be gathered together to form what he called "Army Group Don." The brilliant General Fritz von Mannstein was put in command. A message, which also reached von Paulus, was sent to the Fourth Panzer Army, one of the elements of the newly formed Army Group Don:

CONTACT IS TO BE RE-ESTABLISHED WITH SIXTH ARMY BY ATTACK BY FOURTH PANZER ARMY FROM SOUTH. AIR GROUP FOUR UNDER FREIHERR VON RICHTOFEN WILL HAVE DUAL JOB OF SUPPORTING ATTACK AND SUPPLYING STALINGRAD. HITLER

Later in the day von Paulus got his orders. The Sixth was to "hedgehog itself in."

This was like throwing a dog in the water and telling him to swim. The Sixth was already dug in. Those on the perimeter holding off Russian tanks and infantrymen were in trenches and foxholes in open fields. The men in Stalingrad itself were burrowed into broken walls, into piles of brick, in parts of houses, in back yards and ruined factory buildings. During the remaining days of November and through December about one thousand of them died every day. During January, closer to fifteen hundred died daily of wounds, exposure, starvation or disease.

Goering did start dropping and landing supplies to the Sixth, but it was evident from the beginning that the job could not be done. The airfields were within range of Russian artillery,

German debris at Pitomnik.

and even when Luftwaffe transports on the ground for the quick job of unloading were not hit directly, the runways at Gumrak and Pitomnik were constantly being pocked with shellholes that had to be filled before take-off. Pitomnik was about five miles from the center of Stalingrad.

THE NUTCRACKER

On December 2, the Russians at Stalingrad's front door organized their first attack on what General Rodion Malinovsky said was "an armed camp of prisoners."

Malinovsky's Chief of Staff, General Peter Kotelkov, said before the attack: "They can dig graves for themselves and prepare crosses—or surrender."

Through the first days of December the Germans fought off the attacking Reds. Some supplies were reaching them by air, and by using their last ammunition stores carefully they were able to limit Russian advances; but the German-held semicircle around Stalingrad was always shrinking. It was nibbled at night after night, day after day, in a thousand small wars. One of these small battles occurred before midnight, December 8, in a field less than four hundred yards wide northwest of the city.

Four German squads, of five to eight men each, were spaced across the field defending the line there from shallow trenches. The temperature had hovered above freezing during the day, but by nightfall it had dropped to twenty-eight degrees. The light snow on the ground was wet, and beneath it the earth was unfrozen and wet. The men lay in cold mudholes looking across a bleak field, trying to hypnotize themselves with thoughts of food, warm fires and home—hoping only that no shapes of men or machines would loom out of the dark across that field.

A rumble, at first distant, grew louder. Those who had managed to shiver themselves to sleep were roused, and each of them lay there silently, rifle in hand, straining to look through the blackness. Suddenly ten Russian tanks careened up over a small hill, their tracks digging into the far end of the field. The German squad on the far left and closest to the Russians, because of the angle of the field, scrambled out of its hole without firing a shot and started to run for the protection of a building several hundred yards away in the back of the field. The men were outlined against the white of the snow-covered field; before they had run ten steps, whiplash streams of bullets from the Russian tanks cut them down.

The Russian tanks came on until they were within a hundred yards of the German positions. Only one trench had a heavy weapon—a 37 mm gun—and this was not effective more than half the time against the heavily armored front plates of the Russian tanks.

"Hold fire!" was the order whispered from hole to hole. The best hope the remaining Germans had was that, with the limited vision inside the tanks, the Russians would pass them by in the darkness and be stopped by the heavier artillery pieces of a few German tanks hidden behind a stone wall some distance to the rear.

Whether the Russians saw the Germans or not, they trundled directly towards two of their positions. The young German gunner behind the 37 mm gun could not stand it, and with the Russians less than fifty yards away he opened fire. The 37 mm shell did not pierce or even slow the tanks' advance; the monsters roared closer at full throttle. Two more Germans leaped from their shallow holes to run for it and were dropped, ten pounds heavier than an instant before. The rest crouched into the bottom of their holes, digging desperately with their bare hands to get lower. The Russian tank nearest the hole from which the two men had come cut its speed and came forward, slowly now. The four men left in the hole, crazed with fear but not daring to run, fought to flatten themselves into the ground. The Russian tank crept on until it straddled the saucer-shaped hole. The men below screamed in terror, and suddenly the man at the throttle inside threw the tank into gear and gave it full power. The cleated tracks dug through the snow into the mud, and the tank settled, perhaps a foot, before the driver cut the power. Instantly he threw the machine into reverse and the tracks ground deeper into the mud. Then he spun the machine to the left and to the right. And as it sank deeper, obliterating the shallow trench, its tracks ground through flesh and blood and bones, and the screaming stopped.

The Russians had planned well for the annihilation of the Sixth Army. The strength of the Red Army edged south, from where it had been concentrated in the Moscow area, until Rokossovsky had five armies totaling half a million men between the Don and the Volga. General Chuikov's Sixty-second Siberians, defending Stalingrad from within, were largely evacuated through the back door across the frozen Volga and then sent westward across the river again a few miles north to join the forces hammering at the Germans in Stalingrad out front. It was a strange turnabout for them, because they were fighting now toward Stalingrad over the same territory they had recently defended. If the Red Army had never fired another shot into Stalingrad the men of the German Sixth would have died of starvation and cold before spring, so with time and the weather on their side, the Russians were in no great hurry.

Knowing they had to move fast to save the Sixth Army while it could still help itself, and before the Russian buildup was complete, von Mannstein directed the Fourth Panzer Army to attack from the south and drive the sixty-two miles into Stalingrad to rescue the two hundred thousand men still alive there. Once again, the Germans underestimated the Russian strength.

By December 19 the 6th Panzer Division of the Fourth Army had driven through biting winds and blinding snow to within thirty-two miles of the city, and for a few clear hours during the morning they could actually see movement and the signal flares being sent up by the desperate men along the southern part of the Stalingrad trap. This was as close as anyone ever got to rescuing them. On the twenty-first of December the attack stalled, and during a hastily called Plans Meeting at Panzer Army headquarters everyone agreed that further advance was impossible. The Red Army was rushing them from all sides and the rescue force itself was in imminent danger of being cut off. Without asking Hitler, ignoring what he knew would be his order to fight through, von Mannstein now got a radio message to von Paulus ordering him to prepare to break out towards the rescue force within twenty-four hours. There were, at this time, about twenty-eight generals in Stalingrad with von Paulus, and some of them had already taken preliminary steps toward what they thought was the inevitable order to break out. Every man in Fortress Stalingrad looked forward to only one thing: the order to evacuate this hated city. But von Paulus, the unbending military man, judged correctly that von Mannstein was acting on his own. He sent back a message refusing to move, giving as his reason the fact that his vehicles had gas enough to carry them no more than twenty miles. It is probable that von Paulus would not have moved anyway without a direct order from Hitler. When Hitler heard of von Mannstein's order and the Sixth Army commander's answer, he radioed for an exact figure on remaining fuel supplies. He got an answer to the last tablespoonful within an hour. With his own pencil, Hitler hastily scribbled a few numbers on a pad and from his knowledge of the vehicular strength of the Sixth, arrived at a figure that conveniently supported his prejudgment. He estimated the Sixth's tanks and trucks could move about eighteen miles on the gas they had.

"There you are, Zeitzler," Hitler said. "The Sixth Army will hold. I cannot be responsible for allowing the tanks to become standing targets in the middle of the steppe for lack of fuel."

Early in December, at a supply depot near the Polish border, hundreds of miles from Stalingrad, the Quartermaster General had gathered huge stocks of the good things Germans eat at Christmastime. The larder was especially full because in the goodness of their hearts German procurement officers had taken over the best of what they could find in the occupied countries for their countrymen at the front. There were 3764 cases of wine and brandy; 10,000 pounds of gourmet cheeses from Holland; chocolate; jam; hams and butter from Denmark; and thousands of pounds of rich cake baked on German orders in Poland. All these things were to be a Christmas treat for the Sixth Army.

(It is important to note here that from the time Hitler made his lightning panzer attacks into Poland, France and the Low Countries, the picture of the German Army the world had was that of a mobile fighting organization composed totally of high-speed panzer units equipped with tanks and armored vehicles. The fact is, that while the German Army had thousands of tanks and trucks, many of the soldiers walked, and a high percentage of its artillery pieces were pulled by horses. The Sixth Army had 29,000 horses at its peak, and about 12,000 of these were trapped with the men in Stalingrad.)

On Christmas Eve an order was issued which must be interpreted as having been a greater blessing for the animals than for the men. Six thousand of the emaciated horses were to be slaughtered to provide a Christmas treat for the troops. They were killed, butchered and the hunks stewed for hours in huge pots. The meat was eaten with a special ration of half a pound of bread and the liquid was retained. This "horse soup" was served as the total ration for the following day. And by comparison with the days that followed it was a feast.

Goering's promise that he could bring in five hundred tons of supplies a day (which von Paulus said was two hundred and fifty tons below what was necessary) was not being carried out. During December, the Luftwaffe lost two hundred and seventy-eight transport planes trying to land or take off from the Pitomnik, Gumrak or Stalingradski airfields. Pilots refusing to land had their crews kick supplies out the cargo doors, and much of this was lost. The troops were being issued half a pound of bread as a day's ration, and on December 26 this ration was cut to four ounces—a few slices. The men supplemented this as best they could. First the dogs, then the cats, finally the rats and mice disappeared from the ruins of Stalingrad. The horses, which enjoyed a special protected status, were transferred from the artillery to the service troops in charge of doling out what food there was. A horse was food now, not transportation. A few hundred were slaughtered each day, to provide the thin hot broth to go with the four ounces of bread. Ironically, the ration was comparable to what the Germans were feeding their concentration camp prisoners at Auschwitz and Buchenwald.

The men in the center of Stalingrad were better off in most respects than those on the perimeter. Russian pressure was being applied from outside, and the men there were sleeping in open fields in the bitter cold with nothing over them. The men on the defensive ring would not have dared to sleep if they could have, because white-robed Russian infantrymen, invisible against the snow, were always infiltrating their positions—and in addition there was constant danger of a Russian tank attack. So, far from any service unit, these men hacked flesh from dead horses which had been frozen in the snow for weeks and ate it raw.

Pitomnik, the most active airfield, was the goal of every German soldier. Men dismissed from duty with missing arms and legs dragged themselves along the five-mile road from the city with the mirage of an airlift in front of them. What planes landed were soon loaded with wounded, but there were no organized facilities for getting them to the field. Fourteen thousand men dropped to freeze or bleed to death on the road to Pitomnik, and after a night's snow one bump in the road was the same as another to the truck drivers moving between airfield and inner Stalingrad.

On January 12 Russian artillery started hitting Pitomnik regularly, and that night one Russian tank circled the field. The ground crews fled in panic; by January 15 the field was finally abandoned. Gumrak was overrun by the Russians, and thus the last hope that the Sixth Army could get supplies from outside died. The mirage of rescue dissolved in the eyes of the wounded, struggling along the road to reach the field.

The wounded within the city were no better off. Deep cellars and vaults under the larger buildings were their hospital rooms, but they provided little more than a protected place where the terribly wounded could die slowly in agony, rather than quickly from a mortar blast or a rifle bullet. Lice crawled over the gaping, gangrenous wounds in black swarms. Men dying of diphtheria, tetanus and pneumonia lay side by side on the stone floors with men whose rotting stumps had not been favored with so much as a dirty rag for a bandage. Some screamed and rolled in convulsive death throes but most of them were so near starvation that their pain could not manifest itself in movement; they lay still with

eyes bulging. When someone noticed that a pair of eyes had not opened for a day or two, the man was moved out, presumably dead, with no further check. One German doctor ordered 141 men he judged hopelessly wounded to be lifted out of the cellar and laid for the night in some unprotected place where they could die in the warm glow that supposedly comes with freezing to death . . . although no one who has been through it ever made a report.

Hour after hour there was a frantic exchange of messages between Hitler's headquarters, Luftwaffe headquarters and Stalingrad. Goering could not land a small fraction of the supplies he had promised, and the Sixth demanded to know why. On January 7 von Paulus radioed this message to Zeitzler at Hitler's headquarters:

IF THE FUEHRER'S ORDERS TO DELIVER 300 TONS DAILY IS NOT CARRIED OUT BY THE LUFTWAFFE WE ARE HEADED FOR A CATASTROPHE AND ALL RELIEF MEASURES ARE USELESS. THE ARMY IS STARVING AND FREEZING. IT HAS NOTHING TO EAT OR SHOOT AND CAN NO LONGER MOVE ITS VEHICLES. EVEN IN GOOD WEATHER WITH THE AIRFIELDS CLEARED WHAT IS PROMISED IS NOT DELIVERED.

The most that had been brought into Fortress Stalingrad on any one day was two hundred and eighty tons. This was the peak reached on only one day late in December when one hundred and fifty planes landed, but it was far above the average. On many days no planes landed at all.

To help curb any tendency history has to put down the German Army as being free of the organizational snafus that plagued the armies of other nations, it should be noted that on one occasion during Stalingrad's desperate last days, when men were stewing steppe grass in melted snow for a meal, a Junkers–52 transport plane landed with a ton of marjoram, ten cases of pickles, fifteen typewriters and a dozen cases of contraceptives. It was not what the men had in mind.

THE BITTER END

By January 8 the Russians around Stalingrad had built up their strength to the point where they knew they could move into Stalingrad when they chose, but in war one man behind a wall with a gun can kill a lot of people and temporarily hold up a large force. If the lead tank in a line of tanks grinding down a narrow street is knocked out, for example, that tank has to be removed before the others can proceed. In an attempt to save those few fundred men who would inevitably be killed in routing out every last German, the Russians made an offer. At ten o'clock in the morning, General Rokossovsky sent three aides toward the German lines bearing a white flag of truce. The following message was handed over, to be delivered to von Paulus.

TO COLONEL GENERAL FRIEDRICH VON PAULUS, COMMANDER OF THE GERMAN SIXTH ARMY, OR HIS ASSISTANT, AND TO ALL THE OFFICERS AND MEN OF THE GERMAN FORCES AT STALINGRAD:

THE GERMAN SIXTH ARMY, ELEMENTS OF THE FOURTH TANK ARMY AND UNITS SENT TO THEM AS RE-ENFORCEMENTS HAVE BEEN COMPLETELY SURROUNDED BY THE RED ARMY FORCES SINCE NOVEMBER 23, 1942. ALL HOPES THAT YOUR TROOPS MIGHT BE SAVED BY A GERMAN OFFENSIVE FROM THE SOUTH HAVE COLLAPSED. THE GERMAN TROOPS RUSHED TO YOUR ASSISTANCE HAVE BEEN ROUTED AND ARE NOW RETREATING TOWARDS ROSTOV.

OWING TO THE ADVANCE WESTWARD OF THE RED ARMY, THE GERMAN AIR TRANSPORT FORCE, WHICH FORMERLY SUPPLIED YOU WITH STARVATION RATIONS OF FOOD, AMMUNITION AND FUEL, IS BEING FORCED TO SHIFT ITS BASES FREQUENTLY AND TO FLY LONGER AND LONGER DISTANCES TO REACH YOU. MOREOVER, THE GERMAN AIR TRANSPORT FORCE IS SUFFERING GREAT LOSSES AT THE HANDS OF THE RUSSIAN AIR FORCE. ITS HELP TO THE SURROUNDED FORCES IS BECOMING INEFFECTIVE. YOUR SURROUNDED TROOPS ARE IN GRAVE DANGER. THEY ARE SUFFERING FROM HUNGER, DISEASE AND COLD. THE HARD RUSSIAN WINTER IS ONLY BEGINNING. THE DEEP FROSTS, COLD

WINDS AND BLIZZARDS ARE STILL TO REACH THEIR FULL FORCE, AND YOUR SOLDIERS ARE NOT PROTECTED WITH WARM CLOTHES AND LIVE IN UNHYGIENIC CONDITIONS.

AS COMMANDER YOU MUST FULLY REALIZE THAT YOU HAVE NO POSSIBILITY OF BREAKING THROUGH THE RING THAT SURROUNDS YOU. YOUR POSITION IS HOPELESS AND FURTHER RESISTANCE IS USELESS. IN VIEW OF THE HOPELESS POSITION YOU FACE, AND IN ORDER TO AVOID UNNECESSARY BLOODSHED, WE OFFER YOU THE FOLLOWING TERMS OF SURRENDER:

(1) ALL THE SURROUNDED GERMAN FORCES UNDER YOUR COMMAND ARE TO CEASE HOSTILITIES.

(2) ALL TROOPS, ARMS, EQUIPMENT AND WAR SUPPLIES ARE TO BE TURNED OVER TO US BY YOU IN AN ORGANIZED MANNER AND IN GOOD CONDITION.

(3) WE GUARANTEE LIFE AND SAFETY TO ALL OFFICERS AND SOLDIERS WHO SURRENDER, AND UPON TERMINATION OF THE WAR THEIR RETURN TO GERMANY OR ANY COUNTRY TO WHICH THEY MAY CHOOSE TO GO.

(4) ALL TROOPS WHO SURRENDER WILL RETAIN THEIR UNIFORMS, INSIGNIA AND ORDERS, PERSONAL BELONGINGS, VALUABLES, AND IN THE CASE OF HIGHER OFFICERS THEIR SIDE ARMS.

(5) ALL OFFICERS AND SOLDIERS WHO SURRENDER WILL BE PROVIDED NORMAL FOOD.

(6) ALL WOUNDED, SICK AND THOSE SUFFERING FROST-BITE WILL BE GIVEN MEDICAL TREATMENT.

YOUR REPLY IS EXPECTED BY 10 A.M. ON JANUARY 9, IN WRITTEN FORM, TO BE DELIVERED BY YOUR PERSONAL REPRESENTATIVE, WHO WILL TRAVEL BY PASSENGER CAR, FLYING A WHITE FLAG, ALONG THE ROAD FROM THE KONNY RAILROAD SIDING TO THE STATION OF KOTLUBAN. YOUR REPRESENTATIVE WILL BE MET BY AUTHORIZED RUSSIAN COMMANDERS.

IN THE EVENT OF THE REJECTION OF THIS PROPOSAL BY YOU, WE NOW WARN THAT THE RED ARMY TROOPS AND RED AIR FORCE WILL BE COMPELLED TO TAKE STEPS TO WIPE OUT THE

SURROUNDED GERMAN TROOPS, AND THAT YOU WILL BE RESPON-
SIBLE FOR THEIR ANNIHILATION.

COLONEL GENERAL NIKOLAI VORONOV
Representative of the General Headquarters
of the Supreme Command of the Red Army
LIEUTENANT GENERAL KONSTANTIN ROKOSSOVSKY
Commander of the Don Front

Within minutes Hitler snapped back an answer to the remaining radio receiving unit in Stalingrad:

SURRENDER IS FORBIDDEN. SIXTH ARMY WILL HOLD ITS
POSITIONS UNTIL THE LAST MAN AND THE LAST ROUND OF
AMMUNITION AND BY THEIR HEROIC ENDURANCE WILL MAKE
AN UNFORGETTABLE CONTRIBUTION TOWARDS THE ESTABLISH-
MENT OF A DEFENSIVE FRONT AND THE SALVATION OF THE
WESTERN WORLD.

On January 27 General Rokossovsky's troops drove to the
Volga through the center of Stalingrad and linked up with the
small Russian elements of Chuikov's Sixty-second Siberian Army
which had been left in the city. The northern and southern elements of the Sixth Army were separated, and organized German
resistance ended. Disorganized resistance continued, from hundreds of two- and three-man fortresses formed of anything a man
could hide behind. The last message reaching Stalingrad from
Army Group Don was a classic bit of irony:

COMPANY AND BATTALION COMMANDERS ARE ENTITLED
ON THEIR OWN INITIATIVE TO AWARD THE IRON CROSS 2ND
CLASS AND 1ST CLASS RESPECTIVELY.

The remnants of the once-proud and mighty Sixth were
fighting in small groups and acting, for the most part, without
direction. One group of twenty marched forward out of Stalingrad
and found a gap in the Russian lines. They headed for the open
steppe country. Spotted by German reconnaissance planes, they
were dropped bundles of food and clothing. Eventually, early in
March, one of this group survived to reach a German unit. Some
attempt was still being made to preserve order by die-hard Ger-

man militarists, and as late as January 24 four Wehrmacht privates were shot for stealing bread from a supply cellar. In all, 364 German soldiers were executed by Germans for such offenses before organized food dispensing ended January 26.

With the persistence of a commercial message, Russian radio was broadcasting this message every five minutes:

EVERY SEVEN SECONDS A GERMAN SOLDIER DIES IN STALINGRAD.

Overhead Russian planes were dropping leaflets, one of which bore a picture of Hitler standing over a grave holding an Iron Cross. The inscription said:

I PROMISED YOU LAND AND GLORY. NOW YOU HAVE BOTH.

At about midnight, January 30, a message came for von Paulus. It was word from Zeitzler that Hitler had promoted him to the rank of Field Marshal. Hitler was apparently confident that this would inhibit von Paulus from being taken alive, a fate that no German Field Marshal had ever succumbed to. But von Paulus apparently did not appreciate the subtlety of Hitler's graciousness, because early in the morning of January 31 this simple last message came from Sixth Army headquarters, deep in the basement of a ruined department store in Stalingrad:

RUSSIANS AT ENTRANCE. WE ARE PREPARING DEMOLITION.

The Germans raised a small white rag and Russian soldiers cautiously approached the entrance to the headquarters. German to the end, von Paulus told the Russian soldiers to go back and get a ranking officer to whom he might honorably surrender. In ten minutes the greatest defeat any army in history had ever suffered was over. Russian general officers and a profusion of Red Army photographers rushed to the scene, and von Paulus, haggard but impeccably dressed, emerged to give himself up.

Photographs of the scene were hastily printed. Some were rushed to Moscow. Others were dropped on about 25,000 Germans still holding out on the northern end of Stalingrad, and on February 2, finally convinced that their commander had ceased fighting, they too gave up. The surrender was now complete and unconditional. It was the original of the pattern of defeat that ended at Hitler's bunker near the Brandenburg Gate two years later.

At Stalingrad probably 23 German generals, 2000 officers and about 130,000 soldiers surrendered. These figures are guesses—the Russians never counted and no German who knew ever returned. It has been estimated that 50,000 German captives died in the first two months of captivity during a forced march south to a prison camp. No one but the Russians knew what happened to the rest, and they have never said. Fewer than 5000 veterans of the surrender at Stalingrad were ever returned to Germany. The rest must be presumed dead.

The fascination of war is the story of violent death and the gamelike movements of men by their leaders. It is the ultimate competition. In modern war, the leaders follow. Were this not so, Adolf Hitler would have been marching out in front of the 230,000 men of the German Sixth Army which attacked Stalingrad. He would have died in battle or in captivity, as did all but a handful of these men, because the operation was the single greatest strategic blunder in modern military history. It was the blunder of a mad genius; a mistake of such magnitude and obviousness that it has to be laid to Hitler's insane willingness to let any number of men die in an attempt to satisfy his lust for power. No other army in the world could have accomplished its own destruction so thoroughly, because none but German soldiers would have failed to revolt against an order to march into Hell.

D-DAY

BY THE END OF THE DAY, June 6, 1944, no one knew what had happened along a sixty-mile piece of the French coast between Caen and the base of Cherbourg Peninsula.

Each of the sixty-odd thousand Allied soldiers who landed within the first twenty-four hours knew a small part of the story in intimate detail. Each knew who of their own was shot through the throat, who through the knee. They knew the first names of ten who drowned, five who hung dead on the barbed wire offshore and two who lay unattended, the blood draining from holes in their bodies. They each knew this ridge of sand, that clump of bushes and a few dozen men near them who were exhausted but unhurt. That was about all they knew, and to many of the fighting men the Invasion seemed a hopeless catastrophe.

IN THEIR HEADQUARTERS near Portsmouth, England, forty-three miles across the English Channel from where the fighting and dying were taking place, Supreme Allied Commander Dwight D. Eisenhower and his staff knew how many they had told to go and when they had gone; from them they had received a few hundred small pieces of the story and the wide-angle reports of the fliers and the sailors who had seen the landings from a mile up or a mile out. Although no soldier on Omaha Beach could have believed anyone planned what he had seen that day, it appeared to the men at Supreme Allied Command headquarters that the Invasion was going according to plan.

Behind the beach fortifications, German Field Marshal Gerd von Rundstedt, at his headquarters outside Paris, knew least of all. He had seen no one die, he had no eyewitness reports. Cut off from most of his field commanders by air attacks and paratroop action that had severed their lines of communication, von Rundstedt was so confused and ill-informed about what had happened that by the end of D-Day he believed the attack was a diversionary raid preceding a full-scale landing to take place farther up the French coast in the region of Pas-de-Calais.

LONG BEFORE THE DAY

The Invasion of France in 1944 has, by its magnitude, appropriated for itself alone the designation "D-Day," a term which until then had been used by military people to indicate the date of execution of any major operation. D-Day was by all odds the greatest co-ordinated effort man has ever made toward a single objective. That objective was to open a hole in the German coastal defenses of France and push through a military force strong enough to drive the Germans out of the European countries they had stolen so that those countries could be returned to their rightful owners. While it might be said that D-Day was more than a day, the drama that took two years to write and produce played only one performance: that was on the beaches of Normandy on June 6, 1944.

From the day in May 1940 when the British were driven into the sea at Dunkirk by the overpowering German blitzkrieg through the Low Countries and France, it was apparent that, unless the Nazis were to dominate the world, someday in the future someone would have to storm back into Europe. But things got worse before they got better. The Germans drove deep into Russia, took most of North Africa and were starving out the British with their submarine warfare against trans-Atlantic shipping. In April 1941, U-boats sank 106 ships in the Atlantic. One convoy headed for Russia with Lend-Lease supplies was almost totally annihilated. Ships carrying 400 Sherman M–4 tanks and 200 Lightning P–38 fighter planes went to the bottom in one action. (Later-day archaeologists exploring the ocean floor are going to find a treasure trove of the twentieth century's equivalent of arrowheads there.)

Almost immediately after Dunkirk, the pressure for re-entry into Europe began to build and Americans were willing to help if they could do it with a ten-foot pole. The materials of war were being shipped to both Russia and Britain but the resistance by Americans to active involvement was strong. Their army, still called "a peacetime army" because the United States was not at war until December 7, 1941, was built to a strength of 350,000 men. The Draft Law was passed, and the Army grew to 1,500,000;

but even then men were released when they reached the age of twenty-eight. Just four months before the Japanese attack on Pearl Harbor, Congress managed to pass, by only one vote, the Selective Service Extension Act, lengthening the term of military service beyond one year and permitting units to be sent out of the United States.

In April 1942 Harry Hopkins, President Franklin D. Roosevelt's principal civilian war aide, and Chief of Staff General George C. Marshall went to London. With the United States's world still crumbling in the Pacific—the fall of Bataan and of Corregidor was imminent—they entered into an agreement with the British: from that day forward the end in view of every Allied move would be a cross-Channel invasion and re-entry into Europe. Here were two nations: Great Britain, whose small bomb-battered island home was being strangled by Germany's U-boat blockade, and the United States, which at that very moment could not save a few thousand of its men in the Pacific from a horrible death at the hands of the Japanese, solemnly vowing to take back all of Europe from the greatest armed force ever assembled, Hitler's war machine. It was a decision on the part of their leaders that indicated great confidence in the people of the two nations and presumed their tremendous capacity to build quickly and equip a fighting force that could cross the wide moat between England and the Continent and storm the castle Hitler had made out of Europe.

For the Allies, the war was run by three men and their aides, Winston Churchill, Franklin D. Roosevelt and Joseph Stalin. From the day Hitler moved into Russia, Stalin began asking for a Second Front to take the pressure off his Red Army. As Stalin's demands grew louder and more insistent, with the Germans approaching first Moscow, then Stalingrad, Churchill pointed out that there had at one time *been* a Second Front and Stalin had not seemed concerned when Hitler demolished it. While the German Army blitzed West through Europe and drove the British off the Continent, the Russians enjoyed a nonaggression pact signed with Hitler in August 1939. Until Hitler sent his army thundering across the Russian border, on June 22, 1941, Russia had actually been delivering food and raw materials to Germany. In short, "Where were you when we needed you?"

While it was not sympathy the Allies felt for Stalin, they realized how pressing his needs were and what good military sense it made to open a Second Front as soon as possible. It may be that Stalin's early arrangements with Hitler saved the Allies from disaster. It made them stronger in the face of Stalin's demands than they might otherwise have been, and they would not be pushed into an Invasion before they were ready. In both 1942 and 1943 plans for a "limited" Invasion of France were abandoned. Consideration was given to a plan to take the Cotentin (Cherbourg) Peninsula and hold it, to develop and establish it as a base for a later full-scale operation. Stalin howled when it was not adopted, and British and American private citizens grew restive, but at this point it would undoubtedly have failed.

Good reasons for abandoning a cross-Channel Invasion plan were constantly presenting themselves to everyone. The November 1942 landing in North Africa had been a thumping success and Churchill, among others, never completely dropped the notion that the Allies' major effort should be from the south. Churchill coined one phrase that did more to undermine confidence in D-Day plans than a mountain of logistical paperwork did to support it. His constant reference to the areas north of the Mediterranean as "the soft underbelly of the Axis" planted the notion in the minds of all but the well-informed that it would be a relatively simple matter to come up through the Balkans, approaching Germany from the south. The distance, the rugged Balkan Mountains, the problem of carrying men and materials another thousand miles from the United States to the Mediterranean made that approach anything but "the soft underbelly." But Churchill, the master chessplayer, was looking ahead. He did not want to see the Russians move in and dominate the Balkans after the war.

Despite these delays, the British and Americans were not unaware of the urgency for a landing in France. Time was important for many reasons:

(1) Every day the Invasion was delayed the Germans poured more concrete, set more mines and fixed more guns in place.

(2) People all over Europe were suffering under German domination; in concentration camps they were dying.

(3) The British people had endured great hardships nobly during a long, hard war and American civilians, though newer to privation, were impatient to return to their free, full life. Civilian morale, on whose support the military depended, would not accept delays forever.

(4) While it was the habit of the free press to treat rumors of "Hitler's secret weapons" lightly, Allied commanders knew they were not propaganda only. Rocket-equipped Luftwaffe fighter planes had taken a high toll of British and United States bombers and mysterious activity at the German experimental station at Peenemunde seemed to be tied to equally mysterious launching pads in the Pas-de-Calais Department, eighteen miles from Dover, England. (These hardstands, as it turned out, were prepared for German V–1s. Had their development been three months advanced, or D-Day three months delayed, they might have turned the tide of battle in Hitler's favor as surely as the atom bomb ended the war against Japan. The first V–1, a small pilotless plane carrying the equivalent of a freightcar load of explosives, hit London the night of June 12, just six days after D-Day.)

(5) As the Royal Air Force and the Eighth United States Air Force battered Germany's production, rail and communication centers with increasing force, Germany's ability to fight the titanic war in Russia was being weakened. After the German defeat at Stalingrad, the tide of battle flowed back towards Germany's own borders. If Russia's land forces continued west and became the actual liberators of all Europe, Great Britain and the United States would be left in a weak postwar position and many of the "liberated" nations might find they had been freed from Fascism only to be dominated by Communism. The Anglo-American and Russian alliance was a marriage of convenience and many foresaw the inevitable postwar divorce. British and American soldiers on the scene were essential no matter how effective the bombing became.

Despite the pressing need for quick action, it was evident to

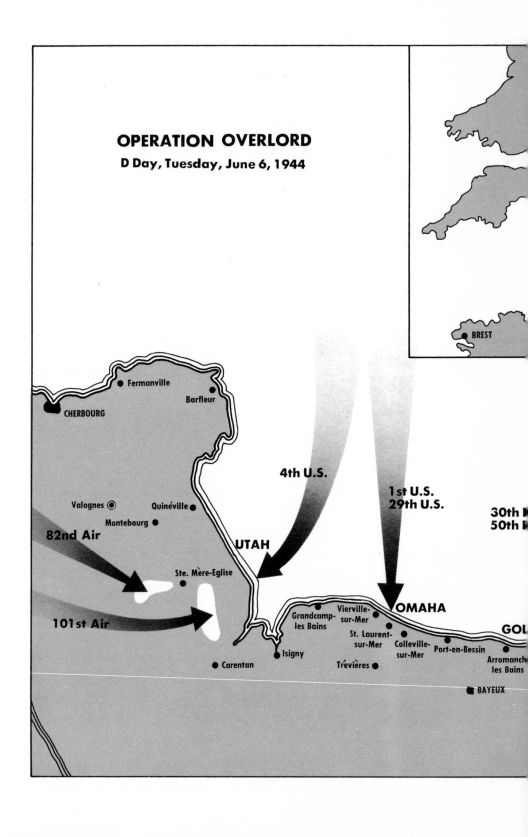

OPERATION OVERLORD

D Day, Tuesday, June 6, 1944

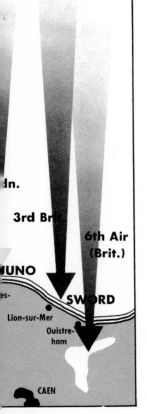

realistic Allied planners that the fall of 1943 was the earliest time by which they could possibly gather together men and equipment enough to give the undertaking any real prospects for success. They not only had to be ready to punch a hole in a heavily fortified coast, they had to have millions of men, and equipment in hard-to-conceive-of quantities, prepared to shove through that hole once it was opened.

The operation was given the code name OVERLORD by Churchill himself, who always took great interest in nomenclature—this romantic little element of war. Details of the interlocking British and American command began to be worked out, and the brillilant British lieutenant general Frederick E. Morgan set out with his staff to lay down the Invasion Plan. It quickly became apparent that fall was no time to go. There was no single day that provided the natural coincidences absolutely vital to a landing. Morgan knew the moon had to rise late to provide darkness for ship and plane movements during the night, and when it rose it had to rise full, to provide light enough for bombers and transport planes carrying paratroopers to choose their drop areas visually. He knew that this moon had to coincide with a tide that was low at an early morning H-hour, so that German obstacles set offshore could be seen by engineers assigned to remove them. The tide, while low, had to be moving in to provide flotation for the landing ships to follow. There was no fall day on which these coincidences obtained. Even if the actual landing could have been successful at that time, it would have meant a winter fight through France to Germany. Difficult weather in war always favors a defender trying to hold, and handicaps an attacker trying to move.

There were, in addition to the Mediterranean possibility, other compelling temptations. By 1943 the air war on Germany was devastating. Many thought this alone would bring Hitler to his knees. British Intelligence also had information about a well-organized plan within the German General Staff to assassinate Hitler. This offered good possibilities of a bloodless end to the war if the Allies could wait it out. The chance of this was considered so good that a plan code-named RANKIN was formulated to move into Germany and take over in the event of a Nazi collapse.

But in the end OVERLORD could not be denied. At the Quebec Conference among Roosevelt, Churchill and their staffs in August 1943 details were discussed, at great length, and it was apparent that there would be no turning back from it. The tentative date for D-Day was set for sometime in May, 1944. It was not until December of 1943 that General Eisenhower learned that he would have the responsibility for the European Invasion. He was, at the time, Allied Commander in Chief North Africa. Roosevelt was returning from the single most important Big Three conference at Teheran, and planned a stopover in Tunis. As theater commander, Eisenhower went there to meet him.

"I was scarcely seated in his automobile," Eisenhower said, "when he cleared up the matter with one short sentence. 'Well, Ike, you are going to command OVERLORD.' "

At Teheran, Stalin had been informed of OVERLORD plans. He agreed to keep as much pressure as possible on Germans at the East Front so that there could be no mass transfers of divisions to France. The only "if" presented to Stalin was in that regard. British and American planners stipulated: "The Invasion will take place *if* not more than twelve German reserve divisions are moved from the East to France." Stalin's tart comment was: "What if there are thirteen—you won't go?"

EISENHOWER TAKES THE BALL

Eisenhower moved into his London headquarters to take charge January 14, 1944. He got most of the top men he wanted, a few he probably did not. His immediate British aides were Air Chief Marshal Sir Arthur Tedder, Admiral Sir Bertram Ramsay, Air Chief Marshal Sir Trafford Leigh-Mallory, and General Sir Bernard Montgomery. His American aides were Lieutenant General Omar Bradley and Lieutenant General Carl A. Spaatz. Brigadier General Walter Bedell Smith, though not technically ranked

The Supreme Commander.

among the top aides, was in all probability the man Eisenhower relied on most in conversation and when seeking the opinion of a friend in whose company he did not have to choose words with diplomatic precision. Both Bradley and Bedell Smith were close personal friends of Eisenhower's. He apparently liked and thought highly of Tedder also and recognized the virtues of Ramsay and Leigh-Mallory. His admiration for Montgomery was somewhat less than boundless. He would have preferred Sir Harold Alexander, but Montgomery had captured the imagination of the British public with his victories over Rommel in the desert and this was a factor to be considered.

The braiding of British and American commands was hard. People got so used to saying Eisenhower knew how to co-ordinate the commands under him and keep people working together that the fact was accepted and forgotten. It was not a negligible factor in the eventual success of D-Day and should not be forgotten. The British and Americans had a lot to offer each other in both attitude and experience, and when each contributed his best talents and stepped aside in recognition of the other's, it was a highly efficient, productive and even happy arrangement. There were, on the other hand, some Americans who loathed anyone and everything British, saying they were pretentious fakes and posturing fops, and there was undoubtedly some of that about elements of the British military. Then, there were British who could not stand Americans, feeling that they were crude, loud-mouthed braggarts, insensitive and without a wisp of cultural background—realistic Americans had been exposed to this charge often enough to suspect it had some basis in fact. And there was one other large group, in each camp, that was as useless to the combined effort as these haters: it consisted of British and Americans who held each other in almost indecent reverence and affection; when there was a difference of opinion, they consistently turned on their own in defense of the other.

Aside from the personal conflicts, there were a thousand details differing for things American or things British. As a particularly nagging example, British war maps were traditionally drawn with enemy lines shown in blue, opposite friendly lines in red. American military maps were the reverse, with enemy in red and friends in blue. Clothing was different; food, and the supply of such luxury items as cigarettes, razor blades, beer and candy, were different. Parts for weapons and vehicles were not interchangeable. While British and American ranks from private to general were more or less equivalent, an American private was paid more than a British lieutenant and there were very few American privates in any headquarters. Most American enlisted men in a headquarters organization where the planning was being done were sergeants of some kind. Except in the infantry, privates were rare, sergeants plentiful. British sergeants were rare. In view of the already great disparity between the rate of pay, even of equal ranks, this proved to be one of the stickiest nonmilitary problems of the pre-Invasion period. The fact was that, with British and Americans living and working side by side, the Americans were living better and the British of equal ability and experience at the lower levels were usually outranked by their American counterparts. For the most part, Americans denied themselves the satisfaction of bending over backwards not to buy their British friends a drink or offer a cigarette and the British for their part did not make a false issue of pride by refusing.

The organizational labor for D-Day was done by these Anglo-American headquarters, but there was no attempt to homogenize the fighting forces, so Americans in the infantry and tank divisions and the large numbers of Air Force personnel had their contact with British civilians in London and in the small villages near their camps. Propagandized in their handbooks to believe the average Englishman was shy, retiring and reluctant to talk, these soldiers were amused to learn firsthand that most Englishmen were not only openly friendly but harder to stop than to start in a conversation. There were the inevitable brawls, and in some areas a bitterness developed; but most Americans who spent this prelude to D-Day in England looked back on it afterwards as their most pleasant interlude of the war. London was a truly big city, the whole island had charm, and they left with the feeling that Englishmen combined the Germans' ability to get things done and the Frenchmen's independent spirit.

THE BUILDUP

The United Kingdom—England, Scotland, Wales and Northern Ireland—is slightly bigger in area than Kansas, not so big as Colorado, and would fit into Texas three times. When the men and machines for the Invasion began to pile into this small area there was lighthearted talk that the British Isles might tip over or sink. By early spring 1944, these forces had been assembled for the fight:

```
     20  United States divisions of 18,000 men each
     14  English or Scottish divisions
      3  Canadian divisions
      1  French and one Polish division
  5,049  fighter planes
  3,467  four-engined bombers
  1,645  two-engined bombers
    698  miscellaneous fighter airplanes
  2,316  transport planes, most of them C–47s (DC–3s)
  2,591  gliders
500,000  tanks, trucks and other military vehicles
```

The total strength of the Allied Expeditionary Force immediately available to Eisenhower in the United Kingdom was 2,876,-439 men, and, just as soon as there was room for them, there were 41 trained divisions waiting to come from the United States. This was a big picnic to pack for.

The initial attack was to be carried out by six infantry and three paratroop divisions, a total of about 126,000 men. Within two weeks after D-Day the Allies planned to put 750,000 men and 95,000 vehicles into France. The problems were supply, movement, secrecy and attack.

Every unit from division to individual fighting man had to be supplied to provide for maximum independence. Every unit had to be equipped to fight with what it had for the first forty-eight hours without asking for anything from anyone. Every soldier had to have about seventy items—weapons, ammunition, clothes, food, water, digging equipment, gas mask, helmet. It was

estimated that one division consumed seven hundred tons of supplies every twenty-four hours.

British roads were generally narrow. A million men and the machines to carry them had to be moved from training areas to British coastal areas with precision, to avoid traffic jams. Their arrival in the port area had to coincide with the arrival of the ships that were to carry them across the Channel. Once the wheels were rolling, if the men arriving in port towns weren't compressed into ships those coming in behind would start to pile up. The movement was too big to stop once it was set in motion. Convoys were best kept moving for many reasons, not the least of which was the strain on Anglo-American relations that inevitably occurred when twenty thousand American soldiers, all with a need for emptying their bladders, pulled to a stop in a quaint English village of a few hundred thatched-roof houses with plumbing no more than adequate for their occupants.

It was no secret to anyone that the Allies were planning an invasion, but it was of the utmost importance that the details of date, time and place be kept from the Germans. With their defensive powers concentrated in one place, there would have been no chance for Allied success. The very size of the OVERLORD plan was helpful. There were so many millions of details that no one man could have given the whole secret to the Germans if he had wished to. Information that necessarily had to be given to unit commanders was doled out in such small pieces that few men had more than a fragment of the picture. Many generals knew only where they were to have their men on a certain date preceding D-Day. They did not know, until they were handed sealed orders on board their Invasion ships, where they were headed or when.

In addition to keeping information from the enemy, we had also to fool them. British Intelligence worked out an ingenious plan code-named FORTITUDE, the object of which was to convince the Germans that the attack was coming in the Pas-de-Calais area. Because the Pas-de-Calais was closest, only eighteen miles from the Dover coast of England, and because its beaches were good, it was the most obvious point of attack. It was an easy matter for German Intelligence, through rejecting the obvious, to take itself back to accepting it for the deceptive qualities of obviousness. The work that went into the Allies' feint at the Pas-de-Calais was, in itself, bigger than any previous Invasion effort, and it was successful in deceiving the Germans beyond an Intelligence agent's wildest hope. The rawboned giant, flamboyant, loud-mouthed, pearl-handled-pistol-packing General George Patton, made one of his most important contributions to the war as an actor in this play. Chosen for his unique talent for attracting attention to himself, Patton was put in charge of what was largely a phantom army in the area around Dover. He had assigned to him many of the divisions which were to follow up the Invasion and they raised such dust in feverish, false-front activity in the Dover area that Luftwaffe reconnaissance planes found them their favorite subject. These photographs were proudly returned to German Intelligence, which predicted that this was the invasion army forming for the attack on the Pas-de-Calais.

FOOLING THE GERMANS

The British had a Patton of their own in General Montgomery. He was hard to hide and the Allies knew the Germans would be watching him. But British Intelligence had a genius for turning German thoroughness and predictability to the Allies' advantage. German antennae in France and Holland were able to pick up many of the radio messages crisscrossing the British Isles and they could pin-point the areas of the greatest communications activity. Montgomery was organizing his troops in his headquarters near Portsmouth to the south. A great number of messages among commands was inevitable but even those going to a sub-headquarters a few miles down the road were relayed, by direct ground wire, one hundred miles northeast to Dover, where a giant radio message center had been built. Every message was sent out from there, leaving the impression on those cocked ears in France that this was the center of the Allied Invasion world.

Light and heavy bombers of the R.A.F. and the United States Eighth and Ninth Air Forces battered the Pas-de-Calais defenses night and day. By the luck of geography, rail lines from Germany through Paris leading to Normandy also fed the Pas-de-Calais area. In strangling the Pas-de-Calais by choking off supplies coming in by rail, the Allies were able to maintain the deception that the attack would come there, and at the same time shut off troop movements and supply trains headed for the true target area in Normandy.

The plan to convince the Germans that attack was coming in the Pas-de-Calais was never dropped by the Allies. On the evening of D-Day a flotilla of thirty-four ships was assigned to tow barrage balloons at low altitudes toward that shore. These shapes, picked up on German radar, gave the impression of an armada headed in that direction. Simultaneously aircraft over the area dropped strips of aluminum foil called, for some obscure reason, "window," to further befuddle enemy radar screens.

In addition to this master plan of deception, hundreds of smaller schemes were devised and executed. There was, for instance, an unknown Englishman whose resemblance to Montgomery was striking. Hearing of this Montgomery double, the British waited until two days before D-Day, then dressed him in a general's regalia and shipped him to Gibraltar on a command aircraft. He arrived in mock secrecy which could not escape the notice of German spies, whose presence in Gibraltar was well known to the British. This information, which was relayed to German Intelligence, was designed to convince them that no invasion of France could be imminent with Monty out of the country.

To provide ultimate secrecy, the coastal area of England where troops were being concentrated was isolated. A ten-mile band was drawn around the island and no civilian without military business could penetrate it. Civilians living there stayed there. To the dismay of such neutrals as Ireland, Portugal, Switzerland and several of the South American countries, all mail and courier message service out of the British Isles was stopped. It was only in April of 1944 that the Allies took this position, that "if you aren't with us, you might be against us."

Allied Intelligence had no good way of knowing how the

Germans were assessing the bits and pieces of false and accurate information they were able to gather, and the matter of making false information hard enough to come by to give it credibility was difficult and delicate. Fortunately the Germans were better at getting the information in the first place than they were at assessing it, and Operation FORTITUDE turned out to be a great success. Nineteen German divisions were tied down in the Pas-de-Calais area waiting for a second attack there—which never came —for several weeks after the Invasion in Normandy.

But the weeks immediately before D-Day were nervous times for the Allied Supreme Command. Invasion maneuvers were executed on British beaches most like those to be hit in France, and for the most part proved a shambles. No one could seriously take any comfort, in this case, from the show-business adage that a poor dress rehearsal presages a successful opening night. Allied officers standing on the cliffs above the simulated landing operation at Slapton Sands shuddered at the thought of what they, had they been German commanders in heavily gunned pillboxes, could have done to the pitifully disorganized landing craft coming ashore.

The most serious incident of the pre-Invasion period came when a flotilla of nine German E-boats ran wild in a convoy of landing ships carrying troops to the practice landing beaches in Devon. The E-boat was a small, fast torpedo-carrying craft somewhat similar to the United States Navy's PT boats. This daring German naval force successfully planted their torpedoes amidship in two of the LSTs, sending them to the bottom of the Channel off the southern coast of England. A third LST was badly damaged. At least 749 men were lost, and "lost" was the word, because the Allied Supreme Command did not know how many of the men had died and how many had been picked out of the water by the Germans. Seven "bigoted" officers were in the maneuver convoy. If the Germans had taken them from the water alive and could wring from them their Invasion secrets, it would seriously jeopardize the landing.

The most dramatic scare was the weird episode involving the crossword puzzle of the *London Daily Telegraph*. In the late

days of May, the solution to this daily puzzle contained several of the Invasion's key code words. Among these were OVERLORD—master invasion plan; NEPTUNE, code word for the D-Day attack plans; MULBERRY, the name given to the cement ships to be towed to the beach area and sunk to provide ready-made harbor and docking facilities; and the words OMAHA and UTAH, the code names of the beach areas marked out for the United States element of the landing force. The puzzles had been worked out for years by an apparently innocent English schoolmaster. When these code names appeared, British Intelligence agents swooped down on Leatherhead, Surrey, where the puzzle expert lived and worked. While it still seems too wild a coincidence to accept, no information has ever been revealed suggesting it was anything but that. British Intelligence, however, does not publicize its successes or its failures, and the whole story may lie buried in its files.

ROMMEL VS. VON RUNDSTEDT

During the Allied buildup, the Germans on their side of the Channel were feverishly trying to fortify their position. Hitler, despite German defeats in Russia, could no longer ignore the imminence of the Allied attack, and he began to move new divisions into France along with increased allotments of supplies. Bastard divisions of captured and impressed soldiers, mostly from Slav units, were formed and equipped with Russian, French and Italian tanks and guns. A few first-class divisions were moved into France along with these, and by June there were a total of fifty-eight combat divisions, about 600,000 men, ready to fight off the Invasion. New emphasis was put on the production of fighter planes, because Allied domination of the Luftwaffe was almost total. This Allied air superiority made transportation close to impossible. During the three months previous to D-Day, the Germans produced 7000 Focke-Wulf 190s and Messerschmitt 109s, but Royal Air Force and United States fighter-supported bombers destroyed them almost as fast as they were made. The German pilot shortage was another insuperable problem. In the spring of 1944 Luftwaffe pilots were being sent into battle with only fifty hours' air time behind them, and they were no match for the expert and seasoned Allied fliers, many of whom had hundreds of hours in actual combat alone. If Luftwaffe pilots escaped destruction in combat, they often died of their own ineptness or from failure of the machines they rode—which had been put together too quickly by inexperienced hands, in factories under incessant bomber attacks. Captured German documents show that in May 712 Luftwaffe planes were shot out of the air and 656 were lost through pilot or mechanical failures.

Since March 1942, when Hitler had appointed Field Marshal von Rundstedt as Commander in Chief, West, the Germans had worked like beavers to build an "Atlantic Wall" that could not be scaled. One German division, for example, labored for two years cutting wood from the Cerisy Forest by hand, hauled it with horse carts to the beaches, and sledge-hammered log fences into the beaches at the high-tide mark. (German gun positions in concrete pillboxes were fixed to cover the beaches at the high-water mark. It was assumed by the Germans that the Allies would come in on flood tide.) In November 1943, the popular German commander of the Africa Corps, the Desert Fox himself, Field Marshal Erwin Rommel, was dispatched to France to supplement von Rundstedt's authority. This produced a confusion of command and defense philosophy that was never resolved. The aging von Rundstedt felt all available German divisions should be concentrated behind the beaches and dispatched to meet the landings when they came. It was Rommel's contention that German strength should be at the water's edge. He repeatedly said that if the Allies were not defeated on the beaches they would not be contained at all. Because he was specifically charged with repelling the Invasion, Rommel redoubled German efforts to make the beaches impregnable. He set about building a continuous defensive belt of strongpoints along the French coast. Every stretch of beach or cliff was covered by several heavy guns. Between these artillery pieces were smaller, fortified machine-gun positions. The fields behind the beaches were heavily mined. The beaches themselves were studded with wood, steel and con-

crete obstacles, startng at the high-tide mark and continuing out into the water. Rommel called for the laying of fifty million mines immediately offshore and farther out in the Channel. German documents reveal that about six million of these were actually set down.

Aware that the Allies were planning parachute and glider landings, Rommel ordered the flooding of any potentially good landing fields. Where flooding was not practical, the Germans set about driving heavy poles into the ground. These poles, eight to ten feet long, were set about fifteen feet apart, less than the wing-spread of any glider. As a final touch, many of these poles were topped with small mines which would explode on contact with any glider or paratrooper. These effective homemade devices were aptly nicknamed "Rommel's asparagus" (*Rommelspargel*) by the Germans.

Despite the efforts the Germans put into all these defenses designed to supplement their heavy gun positions and rolling railroad artillery pieces, the odds were against them. The Luftwaffe had been all but annihilated by the R.A.F. and the Eighth and Ninth United States Air Forces. Low-flying Allied fighter bombers continually plopped explosives on roads, rail lines and bridges. They splattered machine-gun fire on any German units caught traveling in the light of day, and German transportation was a shambles.

One German cavalry battalion, rushing to the Normandy coast from the South of France by train, was attacked by fighter bombers. The train, thirteen cars long, was loaded with men in the first nine cars and horses in the last four. The engineer opened his throttle, as if he could have escaped four-hundred-mile-an-hour planes. One small, well-placed bomb cut the train in two, between the ninth and tenth cars. The cars carrying the battalion

Von Rundstedt inspects the beach defenses.

raced on until they were more than one hundred miles from the detached horse-filled cars. From that day forward these cavalry-men were foot soldiers.

THE SOFTENING-UP

In March the Allies more than doubled their attacks on German rail transportation. The chief construction engineer said he needed two hundred and forty carloads of cement a day to meet his building schedule for the Atlantic Wall, but the Germans couldn't ship cement when they were desperate for weapons, ammunition and food. Colonel Hans Hoeffner, Hitler's rail transportation officer in the West, estimated the six hundred thousand German troops in France needed one hundred trainloads a day for maintenance alone. By the end of March the Allies had destroyed three fourths of the two thousand locomotives on the French rail system in the area; less than twenty trains a day were getting through. In desperation, the Germans took eighteen thousand men off their coastal defense jobs to help repair bridges and rail breaks. That still was not enough. In May the German High Command withdrew another ten thousand men from pillbox construction and assigned them to rail repairs, but it was an impossible job. Fighter bombers and heavy bombers were creating nightmares of confusion in bright daylight. They turned the German Army's day upside-down. No Germans moved by truck, rail, horse or bicycle during the light hours. Track breaks were repaired quickly enough, but the Allies were striking at major switching centers, at locomotive repair depots and at bridges. Often the bridges were hastily repaired so that they would support one freightcar at a time but not a locomotive. The cars were shoved across the precarious bridge one at a time and picked up by another engine on the other side. There were twenty-four road and rail bridges over the Seine River between Paris and the West Wall, and by the end of May all but three were destroyed or so badly damaged they could not be used. The remaining three were under such heavy attack that crossing was suicide. The bridge problem was so acute that General Geyr von

Schweppenburg recommended rebuilding all river bridges a foot or so underwater, so that they would appear to Allied pilots to be useless.

In the three months of concentrated rail attacks that began in March, the Allies reduced German transportation by about 90 per cent. There had been some concern in Allied Headquarters about French civilian reaction, because large numbers of them were killed in these attacks. The Allies estimated an average of one hundred French friends might die in each attack and that a total of eighty thousand might be killed in the campaign against rail transport. No figures are available. Many Frenchmen died, but whatever the number was, there has never been any evidence that the French did anything but hope for more bombers and heavier raids. Their great desire for freedom was never more apparent. They not only accepted the bombing of their own country and inevitably their homes and places of business, but they aided in the destruction of their own rail system with hundreds of major acts of sabotage. In a depot outside Paris, gas was poured into the boiler of a waiting engine, which exploded when it was fired a few hours later. No mile of open track was safe, because French saboteurs took every opportunity to remove sections of track to wreck trains laden with troops and supplies.

THE WALL

Despite all their problems, the Germans were sitting behind a fortified wall with hundreds of heavy guns looking down on the beaches and out into the rough Channel water over which the Allies had to bring their attacking force. Hitler had sixty divisions in France and the Low Countries and all but three of these were close enough to the coast so that their heavy artillery could reach the beaches. In the Normandy area alone, the Allies knew Rommel and von Rundstedt had eight 170 mm guns each of which was capable of throwing a two-thousand-pound shell sixteen miles. The fields above the beaches were planted with mines that would blow the track off a tank or the leg off a man. The crude obstacles placed just offshore, to slow or stop landing craft,

were backed up on the beaches with thick rolls of barbed wire. If the artillery didn't blast the landing craft out of the water when they stopped for the obstacles, Rommel figured German riflemen and machine-gunners would drop the invading infantrymen when they came to the barbed wire. In many beach areas heavy artillery pieces were concealed in blockhouses sided with clapboard and topped with a thatched roof, as if they were innocent French peasant homes. On the coast near Le Havre, hundreds of miles of piping had been laid down on the beach. Built like an overhead sprinkling system, this devilishly clever system of pipes led back to concealed oil tanks. Within seconds the Germans could flood the beach with oil and turn it into a flaming inferno.

"I am looking forward to the battle with confidence," Rommel said in a letter to his wife.

ALLIED INGENUITY

Had Rommel known the extent of Allied preparations, he might not have written so confidently. The attack was being mounted not only in great strength but with considerable ingenuity. Drop-ramp landing craft, developed largely by the British and produced in the United States, were ready to take tanks, trucks and men close into the beaches. (The smaller landing craft were not able to make the rough, cross-Channel trip and were loaded aboard larger ships.) These armored, shallow-draft carriers were a great improvement over the barges and conventional craft previously used for assault purposes. Tanks, principally the American Sherman M–4, had been modified in every conceivable way to produce half a dozen models designed for special work. One model had been built without a top turret so that it could be driven into shallow gullies to provide a bridge over which others could pass; another group was built with flailing chains attached to a drum that revolved in front of

German soldiers block the streets in towns behind the beaches.

the tanks to explode mines before weight of the body of the tank reached them; others were designed with giant flame-throwing devices in place of their guns. The most important re-design of the Sherman was called the "DD" (Duplex-Drive) or amphibious tank. The British Admiralty had seen this invention of the Hungarian-born engineer Nicholaus Strassler, and was certain this tank with a canvas hoopskirt filled with air could never swim in open water. But enough people were convinced of its possibilities for it to be demonstrated to Eisenhower on January 27, 1944. The following day Eisenhower dispatched a British engineer to Washington with blueprints for the conversion, and within two months three hundred Sherman tanks had been altered, equipped with propellers, and shipped to England.

The dukw ("duck"), an amphibious two-and-a-half ton truck, had been provided the Invasion forces, but standard vehicles were necessary also, and from experience Allied commanders knew that landing craft could not push in close enough to the beaches to drop vehicles on dry sand. To make certain the fewest number of vehicles drowned in four or five feet of water, soldiers waiting for the attack spent thousands of hours waterproofing them. This was accomplished by covering every engine part with a specially prepared wax and affixing a snorkel to the carburetor to provide air. A jeep properly prepared could actually travel a short distance on the Channel bottom, covered with water.

Allied soldiers were the best-equipped attacking force ever assembled. Much to their own disgust, they were even prepared against a gas war. The clothes they wore were impregnated with a greasy protective substance designed to make them impervious to mustard gas, and they were all issued masks.

THE DILEMMA

They found the gas masks cumbersome to carry and the clothing uncomfortable, but Allied commanders were taking no unnecessary chances. By the end of May it was apparent to everyone in the British Isles that little more could be done to insure the success of the Invasion Force—it had to be put to the test.

Eisenhower had been given a promising weather forecast for the first week in June by Chief Meteorologist Group Captain J. M. Stagg, and the Invasion was set for Monday, June 5.

"We have almost an even chance of having pretty fair conditions," Eisenhower wired General George C. Marshall in Washington. "Only marked deterioration would change our plans."

With the Invasion two days off, the weather did deteriorate, and Eisenhower was faced with a historic dilemma. The 4 A.M. forecast on the morning of June 4, for the following day, indicated the probability of high winds and low clouds. Low clouds would make visual air support impossible and the predicted waves of from ten to twelve feet in the Channel would swamp small landing craft and make fire from big naval guns on pitching battleships wildly inaccurate.

Eisenhower made the immediate decision to delay the Invasion one day, but he knew this was the limit. All troops had been on board their ships since June 3, and many vessels had been loaded since May 30.

On June 6 tide and moon conditions were more or less the same, but more than a day's delay would mean chaos. The next coincidence of proper moon and tide was a month off. In addition, there was the promise to Stalin, there was the need for every day of fighting time in France before winter, and there was the delicate matter of troop morale. Could they stand being unloaded and shipped back to camp areas for another month of sweating it out? And if they were sent back to the camps they had just left, where would the men behind them who had moved into these camps be sent?

"The inescapable consequences of postponement were almost too bitter to contemplate," Eisenhower said.

Again at 4 A.M. the following morning, June 5, Eisenhower and his staff met with the weather experts. It was one of those days when you had only to look out the window.

"Our little camp was shuddering under a wind of almost hurricane proportions," Eisenhower said. "It seemed impossible that in such conditions there was any reason for even discussing the situation."

The stunning news presented at that meeting of damp commanders came from Stagg. There would, he predicted, be a period of about thirty-six hours of reasonably good weather in the Channel beginning early in the morning of June 6, after which it would very probably worsen again. The prediction for waves in the Channel of four to six feet and scattered clouds covering about half the sky was hardly ideal. Air Chief Marshal Leigh-Mallory was pessimistic about the ability to provide good air support with these cloud conditions, and he felt paratroopers might be dropped to certain death far off their target areas if transport pilots could not see their landmarks below. The prediction for worsening weather after thirty-six hours was a further complicating factor. Once the beachhead was established, the men would need supplies and re-enforcements in great quantity. If weather prevented these being delivered, the Germans might push the invaders back into the sea.

The look on Eisenhower's face during this fateful moment of decision in the library of Southwick House where this meeting took place has been variously described, but his exact words were set down in notes made at the time by Air Vice Marshal James M. Robb.

"The question is," Eisenhower said, "just how long can you hang this operation on the end of a limb and let it hang there?"

After perhaps seven or eight tense, silent minutes Eisenhower had made up his mind.

"I'm quite positive we must give the order. I don't like it, but there it is. I don't see how we can possibly do anything else."

The greatest armada ever assembled, 5300 vessels, reared and plunged toward France through the dark rough waters of the English Channel as midnight approached on June 5. The men on board were miserable in their cramped quarters. Many of them were sick and the understanding ones were afraid. Some were both sick and afraid. Back of them in England, the first of 19,000 airborne soldiers were being loaded onto transport planes for the drop behind the beaches. The Planners had plotted the fight and handed it over. The younger men had to do it.

There were five code-named beaches in the sixty miles between Caen and the elbow of the Cotentin Peninsula: Sword, Juno, Gold, Omaha and Utah. The British 3rd and 50th Divisions on Sword and Gold were split by the Canadian 3rd Division going in on Juno. The United States 1st Division, which had already seen more than its share of the war, was assigned Omaha, along with elements of the 29th Division, and the United States 4th drew Utah, in the crook of the peninsula.

The Royal Marines were given the job of filling the four-mile gap between the British and Canadian beaches. Omaha and Utah were split by a miniature Gibraltar, Pointe du Hoc, and two specially trained Ranger Battalions, the 2nd and 5th, were asked to scale its abrupt hundred-foot rock cliff and destroy the heavy German artillery guns dominating both beaches.

Immediately behind these first waves were the British 49th Division, the 51st Highland Division, and the 7th Armored Brigade, the rest of the United States 29th and the United States 2nd and 90th Divisions. The rugged British 6th Airborne was assigned the drop zone, behind Sword along the Orne River between Caen and the beach. They were to take bridges and hold off strong German forces that could be sent from the Pas-de-Calais until more British forces got ashore. The tough United States 82nd and 101st Airborne Divisions were to drop inland at the base of the Cotentin Peninsula nearest Utah. Including naval personnel and fliers, the Allies were using half a million men for this one day's battle. It was hoped that as many as 120,000 would get ashore in the first twenty-four hours.

No one cares about the names and numbers of fighting units except the men in them, and they don't care about any others. It is difficult to get the whole story of a battle from the men who were there for this reason, and also because, for the most part, they don't know the story. Soldiers seldom agree with the place history gives them in the picture of the operation drawn after the battle is over. It did not seem that way to them. D-Day was a battle that clearly changed the course of history, but close up there was nothing clear about it. The story is a hundred thousand incidents, and while each one influenced all the others, it is guesswork to suggest which ones were related and in what way. The following narration, from the time the first paratroopers dropped into Normandy at about 12:15 A.M., June 6, consists of a few hundred bits and pieces of the facts. From them it is possible to understand something of what happened.

THE JUMPERS

There were clouds over the coastal areas of Normandy and the moon did not light the earth below except in isolated patches. Transport pilots flying the eight hundred and five C–47s carrying United States paratroopers had never been over France before, and had never been shot at by flak batteries below. It was difficult to locate the drop areas in the darkness; and when the antiaircraft fire became intensive the pilots gained altitude, changed their course, flew faster and took violent evasive action to avoid being hit. The C–47s were slow, but even at one hundred and twenty miles an hour a plane moves across miles of land in a few minutes. They were crossing the Cotentin Peninsula from west to east, dropping their loads and heading back across the English Channel.

Eighteen men, the oldest twenty-six, sat in the benchlike seats lining each side of the C–47. Each man had strapped to him a rifle, ammunition, grenades, a piece of a machine gun or a bazooka, a gas mask, K-rations for two days, shovel, knife, and in his pocket ten dollars in new United States-made French money. In addition to his own weight and the parachute which was to float him to earth, each man was carrying about eighty pounds of equipment.

In the cockpit the pilot, navigator and flight engineer pored over a map, looked anxiously below. They were not sure, but they had to make a decision. The word was passed and the paratroopers stood. The jump sergeant kicked open the door. It was the moment eighteen men had trained three years for. One by one, at ten-second intervals, the eighteen men bailed out. Their chutes opened and in darkness they floated down. A few hundred yards apart, in a perfect line of dots, eighteen strong young men died screaming in the last few seconds of life as they drowned in the English Channel.

Paratroopers were scattered all over Normandy. Tangled in the shrouds of their chutes, many dangled helplessly from the limbs of trees high above the ground and were shot like birds by German gunners below. In the target town of Ste.-Mère-Église, Private John Steele's billowing parachute caught the steeple of St. Vincent de Paul's church. For two hours Steele hung there in his shrouds as though dead so that he would not be riddled with bullets. Miraculously, he was not. Others, loaded with ammunition, grenades and explosives, dropped onto burning rooftops and were blown apart as the arsenal strapped to them exploded.

Paratroopers who landed safely in the darkness took from their pockets the war's cheapest, and one of the most effective, instruments of communication. A small dime-store cricket, the traditional table favor of an American child's birthday party, had been given to every trooper. The signal was one *click clack* of the cricket to be answered by a double *click clack, click clack*. This simple toy enabled hundreds of isolated paratroopers to separate friends from enemies in the darkness.

Through the first night the rules of war were suspended. The Germans took few prisoners, and word of atrocities spread to both sides. The paratroopers were tough, they had been taught to fight dirty, and none of them who saw the riddled bodies of companions hanging from trees were inclined to accept a surrender gesture from any group of Germans; and, regardless of how they felt, it was not practical for a small, detached squad of lightly armed men to take prisoners when they were deep inside enemy territory. One of the first victims of this no-quarter war was the German commander of the 91st Division.

The 91st was a floating division in the Cherbourg area, specifically trained to fight airborne landings. Late in the evening of June 5, General Wilhelm Falley left for an important meeting with other staff and division officers in Rennes. As Falley's driver headed for Rennes, the general became concerned over the extraordinary air activity he could see behind him toward the coastal area he had left. Ordering his driver to turn around, Falley raced toward his headquarters at the Château Haut, north of the small town of Picauville. As his car careened to a halt in the courtyard near daybreak, General Falley stepped out and was shot dead by a small patrol of United States paratroopers.

General Matthew Ridgway, the able commander of the 82nd Airborne, said the lieutenant in charge of the patrol reported the incident to him with great glee. At the time, Ridgway's own position was precarious. He had set up a headquarters of sorts in an apple orchard at an uncertain distance from enemy units on four sides.

"Well," Ridgway said to the lieutenant, "in our present situation, killing division commanders does not strike me as being particularly hilarious, but I congratulate you. I'm glad it was a German division commander you got."

British and American gliders were built, like orange crates, to be used once and abandoned. The plan called for them to come in shortly after the paratroopers had landed, bringing re-enforcements and heavier equipment. The troopers needed jeeps, ammunition and the 57 mm antitank guns that could be brought in by glider. The 82nd Airborne was to be bolstered by four thousand glider-borne infantrymen at the first light of dawn. The gliders came all right but most of the landings were little better than a bad plane crash. The mists rising from lowlands obscured landing fields and in many cases there were no fields to land in anyway.

They struck trees, broke in pieces and spilled the men in them to the ground, often dead and usually badly hurt.

They careened into fields planted with Rommel's posts and were made cigar-shaped as they were shorn of their wings.

Some landed in clear plots, plowed through small groups of cows, and flipped over on their backs as they hit the hedgerows at the end of the fields.

They plopped down in the swampy areas of the Merderet and Douve Rivers, where both men and equipment were sucked

down into the muck. The glider landings were largely disastrous, but some men lived to fight and some equipment was salvaged.

BRAVE AND BRITISH

Aerial photos of the French coast revealed hundreds of German strongpoints that had to be reduced before H-hour. One of these was a German gun position at Merville, which dominated the British beach just west of the point where the Orne River flowed into the Channel. Months in advance, the assignment was given to a battalion of British paratroopers commanded by Lieutenant Colonel Thomas Otway. From the pictures and from Intelligence reports, Otway knew this much about it: Four 150 mm guns poked from the protection of re-enforced concrete bunkers four feet thick; the bunkers were surrounded by trenches manned by 180 German soldiers armed with machine guns; beyond the trenches a heavy barbed-wire entanglement encircled a minefield one hundred feet deep.

The original plan was for one hundred Lancaster bombers to hit the revetments shortly before the paratroopers moved in. Otway was willing but he felt the mission was suicidal as planned. A replica of the installation was built in England, and, after studying details of the attack, Otway hit on a daring, dangerous scheme. When the heavy bombers had finished plastering the gun position, three Horsa gliders carrying about thirty men each would land almost on top of the bunkers, inside the ring of barbed wire. Simultaneous with the glider landings, Otway's battalion would attack on foot. The plan was set and rehearsed five times, gliders and all.

On D-Day Otway and his men dropped from their transports shortly after one o'clock and from the beginning almost nothing went right. The battalion was scattered over thirty miles of France. Five gliders accompanying the paratroopers with jeeps and antitank guns were cut loose miles short of their target area and disappeared into the Channel. Two hours after the landing Otway had assembled only one hundred and fifty men from his battalion with one machine gun among them and barely enough explosives to blow up the battery even if the bombers had done their job. The gliders were scheduled to come in on top of the bunker at 4:30 A.M. Otway and his men were still more than a mile from it, and he knew he had to get moving if they were to be there at all. The troopers stopped their search for weapons and explosives dropped by parachute and set out through the night for this most dangerous mission.

The bombers had come and gone when Otway's party reached a point near the Merville battery. They had not dropped a bomb within half a mile of their target. At precisely 4:30 the Halifax bombers with two of the three Horsa gliders in tow appeared overhead. Otway was helpless. His flares were lost and he could not send up the signal. One glider disappeared into the night and Otway saw the second skim in over the gun battery and crash several hundred yards away.

The first streaks of light were beginning to appear in the east, and Otway knew his force of one hundred and fifty men had to do it alone now, and quickly. With three bangalore torpedoes they had salvaged, the British troopers blasted openings in the barbed wire and in the face of withering machine-gun fire and certain death if they hit one of the many mines buried in the ground, they raced across the one hundred yards toward the bunkers. Those Englishmen who made it across the field fell into the trenches on top of the Germans behind the machine guns. In the short, vicious hand-to-hand fight that followed, the Germans were no match for the cream of England's army. Many were shot, stabbed, or strangled, and the rest surrendered. Half of Otway's battling band of one hundred and fifty lay dead with the Germans, but the guns of the Merville battery were silenced. Plunging across the Channel, several thousand men about to land on the beach below owed arms, legs, lives to those who lay dead. But there was no way for them to know.

EFFECTIVE CHAOS

While the paratroop and glider landings seemed chaotic to the men themselves and to the Allied leaders trying to fit them into an orderly report, they were strangely effective. They were, in fact, chaotic, disorganized and in many cases disastrous, but their lack of orderliness confused the Germans more than did the Allies. In a dark house, the intruder downstairs has the advantage of plan and surprise. The Allies were the intruder, and the Germans did not know when, where or by what force they would be struck. German soldiers were terrified of Allied paratroopers—and well they might have been, because these men, so quick to feed a stray puppy, were at the same time well-trained, physically perfect cutthroats. British paratroopers had spent some time learning the very best way to cut a throat. The knife, a special knife made by the famous swordmaker Wilkinson, was inserted from the side just above the Adam's apple and about an inch deep. With the blade all the way through, a quick backward jerk on the handle, using the tough chords at the side of the neck as a fulcrum, cut both the trachea and the major artery in the throat. It was quieter than a bullet, very quick, and the knife could be re-used repeatedly without adding, as more bullets would have, to the trooper's initial jump weight.

The Germans tried to organize to counterattack the paratroopers, but this was the type of Indian warfare the Germans were traditionally unable to cope with: small groups moving on their own initiative, a style of fighting at which Americans in particular were unexcelled.

Paratroopers cut every wire they found, and French Resistance fighters worked to isolate every German headquarters. The Allies added to the confusion by dropping several hundred dummy paratroopers far to the south of their actual landing zone. These dummies were equipped with firecrackers fused to start popping when the dummies hit the ground. It was one of the many small deceptions that made the Germans uncertain about where the main attack was coming and thus made it impossible for them to throw the weight of their floating divisions in any one direction.

In a hundred little battles the paratroopers were successful, although it did not seem so to them at the time. One regiment of the United States 101st was to seize the lock at La Barquette. The Germans were using the lock to back up the Douve and Merderet Rivers, in order to make swamplands of many inland fields. (A swamp was as effective as several concrete blockhouses in preventing the movement of tanks and men.) Although the entire officer staff of one of the battalions of the regiment was lost in the drop, and most of the regiment was widely scattered, the regimental commander, Colonel Howard R. Johnson, collected about one hundred and seventy men and set out toward the river lock. They were successful in capturing the position and met relatively little enemy resistance, so Johnson left one hundred men to protect what they had already won and set out to get the bridges farther west along the Douve. Johnson met another fifty troopers who were engaged in a hard fight with major elements of a strong German division in the area. With small radio equipment, he was able to contact naval forces offshore and to direct heavy fire on the enemy from the eight-inch guns of the heavy cruiser *Quincy*.

Because of the scattering and the losses in the drop, the strength of both the 101st and the 82nd was far below what it should have been for every action planned. A battalion was a company now, a company was a platoon, and a squad was any two men together.

At the little town of Chef du Pont, Captain Roy E. Creek was left to protect that position with about thirty-five men. Early in the morning a strong German unit moved in across the river. With nothing left but small arms and precious little ammunition, Creek and his small crew knew they would be wiped out unless they got re-enforcements. Creek radioed for help, but the nearest paratroopers were four miles away at La Fiere, and there was no certainty they could make it in time or even at all. The paratroopers were generally critical of the help they got from the glider forces, but it was at this moment that a C–46 roared overhead towing one of the maligned orange crates. The glider slipped her towrope and landed a few hundred yards from Creek's position. There were twelve airborne infantrymen aboard her, and a blessed antitank gun. With these re-enforcements, Creek's men

were able to hold off the German counterattack. Other re-enforcements, about one hundred men, did actually arrive about an hour later. With this force Creek took the offensive, drove the Germans from the east bank of the river and dug in there.

This is the way the war went for the paratroopers.

THE WAIT OFFSHORE

While the paratroopers groped their way through the darkness inland, killing, dying and raising havoc, the great gray fleet of transport ships anchored ten miles offshore. Infantrymen started scrambling down the broad net ropes into the small landing craft bouncing at their sides. Each infantry company in the first assault wave loaded into six boats, thirty-two men to a boat. The craft were loaded front to back according to this plan: six riflemen, each carrying ninety-six rounds of ammunition, up front behind the ramp; a team of four wire cutters; four men with two Browning Automatic Rifles and eighteen hundred rounds of ammunition; two bazooka teams of two men each; a four-man mortar team with a 60 mm mortar and twenty rounds of ammunition; a two-man flame-thrower team; five demolition men with TNT; a platoon or section leader; and one officer. The last man in the boat was the medic.

Each man carried raincoat, shovel, gas mask, five grenades, a small block of TNT, three boxes of K-rations and three of the more concentrated D-rations. Every man wore a life preserver; some wore two.

Two hours before H-hour, 6: 30 A.M., the sea in the Bay of the Seine was dotted with hundreds of small Invasion craft. The sky was streaked with light now, and the men in the boats felt some protective comfort from the roar of the bombers overhead. A thousand R.A.F. Lancasters had dropped their loads in the night and at the first light the heavy bombers of the United States Air Forces came in. There were scattered clouds and the infantrymen might not have felt so comforted had they known the bombers were ordered to delay their instant of bomb release by thirty seconds, but with limited visibility this was insurance against

bombs being dropped on the invading forces. The extra thirty seconds, however, carried the bombers across the coast and inland, where most of their bombs dropped well behind the German gun positions they were supposed to blast.

Far offshore the seas rose to heights of six feet and the small landing craft shuddered as their square bows hit every wave. The men who were not sick had taken so much dramamine they were sleepy. Sheets of cold water poured into the boats, and many of the men sat in six inches of water retching miserably over themselves and one another. In some of the boats men bailed with their helmets as the water level rose.

Forty-five minutes before the touchdown, big guns of the British and United States Navies boomed out. The men in the boats were encouraged again by the arc of fire thrown over their heads by these great batteries of floating artillery. It made it seem less as though they were going in alone. As yet there was no answer from the German batteries on shore, and a wild hope was entertained: Had they all been knocked out?

THE DAY THEY DIED

To several thousand Americans Omaha is not a city—it is a six-mile-long, crescent-shaped beach in Normandy. Not all the fighting took place there on D-Day, but Omaha was the most important and the bloodiest of the five code-named beaches. The invasion at Omaha was a series of disasters that added up to a success. It was the re-enactment of the nightmare every Allied commander and every invading soldier had dreamed. Everything happened that anyone ever feared might, and some things happened that were beyond the imagination's ability to forecast.

Two hundred landing craft started for Omaha carrying eight companies of infantrymen and an engineer demolition task force of 272. There were 96 tanks to support the infantrymen, and of these 64 were the amphibious DDs, capable of swimming ashore under their own power. At least that's the way it had worked in training. There were four DDs on each of the sixteen LCTs that had crossed the Channel on their own bottoms. Each of the tanks weighed thirty tons. When the tank was in the water, supported by the flimsy air-filled canvas waterwings attached to it, only the turret protruded. The tank commander stood on a platform behind the turret, but the four other members of the crew sat sweating in the cramped quarters below the water in this ill-conceived submarine.

The flotilla of LCTs with the amphibious tanks was under the command of a naval lieutenant named Dean Rockwell. He dispatched eight of the craft to the eastern end of the beach while he stayed on one of the eight LCTs to the west. The plan had been to launch the DDs 6000 yards offshore, so that the big LCTs would not become targets for German short batteries. In the water the DDs themselves offered little to shoot at. Rockwell looked apprehensively at the waves, many of which were five feet high even near shore. It was his judgment that the tanks could never make it and he made the abrupt decision to ignore orders and carry the tanks close in on the landing craft.

The command decision on board the LCT at the eastern end of the beach was less wise. At H-hour minus 50 minutes, with the craft more than a mile from land, the order was given for the tanks to go. The ramps of the eight LCTs dropped and in each one the first of four tanks trundled forward and waddled into the sea. It was the beginning of the indescribable disaster at Omaha. One tank nosed off the carrier and as a wave lifted the bow of the ship the end of the ramp caught the tail of the steel monster and flipped it turret-down into the sea. Tank after tank crawled off the ramps into the Channel. In many cases, their billowing canvas life jackets were ripped. Some of them paddled a few hundred yards and slowly sank under the waves. Most of them foundered as soon as they were launched and dropped to the bottom of the English Channel like lead weights, with no sign except a frantic bubbling as water replaced air in the tanks and in the lungs of the men trapped there. Terror? This far end of the Detroit production line that had produced these Sherman tanks was a devil's joke.

Within five minutes of the order to launch, 27 of the 32 tanks had plunged to the bottom. A handful of crewmen bobbed in the water. The rest of the 135 men died clawing to get out. Five tanks reached the beach. Two got in under their own power, and three were brought in by an LCT commander who refused to send off the last three tanks after he watched the first one go down.

Rockwell, meanwhile, led the eight LCTs under his direct command to within fifty yards of dry beach. The Germans, who had held their fire for so long, were banging away now at ships and tanks. By the time all thirty-two tanks were unloaded, two of Rockwell's LCTs were burning and a third was riddled at the waterline with shell blasts. But their tanks were on the beach.

In the year 2000, anyone interested in the recent history of the world will be able to see almost any event that took place after 1930 on film or tape—but they'll have to read about the great battle that took place on D-Day, because few still photos and almost no motion pictures were taken where the fighting was going on. There are pictures of what it was like just before the battle and there are pictures of what it was like just after. There are pictures that indicate the magnitude of the battle, and pictures taken at some of the landing areas where there was relatively little enemy opposition. No one was taking pictures on the Dog Green sector of Omaha when Able Company came in.

There were seven boats when they left the side of the transport. One man lay in the bottom of No. 3 with a leg that had been mashed flat from above the knee when it was caught between the steel sides of the *Thomas Jefferson* and the gunwale of his landing boat. There was nothing to do but take him along.

The wind was twenty miles an hour, the waves from three to six feet high. A few minutes after 6 A.M., with the boats still more than two miles offshore, the German gun batteries opened up. For a while their shells plopped harmlessly into the Channel, far short. At about 6:15, half a mile offshore, Boat No. 5 took a direct hit. The fluffy kapok stuffing flew like chicken feathers from the life jackets of men who had been blown to pieces. The boat settled quickly into the water and the men, who had more equipment hooked to them than their life jackets would float, went down with it. Second Lieutenant Edward Gearing and per-

haps half of the men were rescued by nearby boats. Gearing himself was picked up by a naval vessel which was not headed for the beach. This made the young lieutenant one of the handful of living members of the 116th Regiment by the end of the day.

As the remaining six boats came in, the heavy artillery seemed to concentrate more on the larger landing craft and on the tanks struggling to get ashore. The six boats were still together, one hundred yards from the beach, but it was too good to last. A shell crashed into Boat No. 3 at the waterline. Two men were killed, and as water rushed in the others fought their way up over the sides to get out. Twelve of them drowned and the rest dropped their weapons, cut away their equipment and devoted themselves to surviving. They were no longer attackers. This left five boats in Able Company of the 116th Regiment.

Machine-gun bullets were rattling off the high sides of the bargelike landing boats now. Their engines were loud, but through the drone of the airplanes overhead and the thunder of naval artillery behind them, the men inside the five boats could hear the screams of those drowning around them.

At 6:36 the ramps dropped and bullets which had been splattering against the front of the Higgins boats poured in. The Germans on the bluffs three to five hundred yards away were shooting down the throats of the open-mouthed landing boats. The men started out in three files, left, right, center. Most of them were shot down before they could go ten feet. Some of them were dropped on the ramp. In Boat No. 2, Lieutenant Edward Tedrick was shot through the throat as he jumped from the boat. He struggled through the water and fell gasping on the beach. Private Leo Nash heard Tedrick gurgle through the blood in his throat "Advance with the wire cutters!" The wire cutters, along with heavy radio equipment, BARs and heavy explosive packs, had been dropped in the water. Many of the men had nothing but their Garand M-1s and some of them had even dropped these. To give the command Tedrick had raised himself from the shallow hole he had found and an instant later Nash saw machine-gun bullets kick across the sand lengthwise, on through Tedrick's body.

The thirty men from Boat No. 1 and another thirty from Boat No. 4 were unloaded in water ten feet deep. Half of them drowned or were killed by the machine-gun fire lacing the water before they reached the beach. Some of the wounded managed to drag themselves to the water's edge, but the tide was coming in fast now and many of these wounded, exhausted men gave up and drowned in a few inches of the English Channel.

No one knows what happened to Boat No. 6, but there is no evidence that any of its thirty men ever reached the beach. It was last seen about one hundred yards offshore and it probably received a direct hit from a heavy mortar or artillery piece.

The only officer of A Company to reach the beach and live was Lieutenant Elijah Nance, and he was hit in the heel as he left his boat and again in the stomach as he waded ashore. Every platoon sergeant was killed or wounded within the first few minutes on the beach, and no one in Able Company had fired a shot in return. The last of the seven Higgins LCAs carried medical corpsmen and one doctor. The ramp of this craft dropped open directly in front of two German machine guns in a pillbox on the bluff. Within seconds, all aboard were dead or seriously wounded. None reached the beach.

The men who had reached the beach from the other boats found that they could not stay there and they could not move forward. Neither naval guns nor aerial bombardment had hit the beach itself, so there were no holes to hide in. Some of the men lay flat in the sand at the water's edge. They did not move and if they were lucky the Germans above could not tell them from the dead on their left and right. Others dropped their uniforms, all equipment including their helmets, turned on their backs and, with nothing but their noses as a snorkel, inched in with the tide.

In some areas men who had reached the beach moved back into the water and hid behind German obstacles there. The wrecked tanks or boats in the shallow waters were poor protection, because they tended to draw the heavy artillery fire. The bravest men who could still move tried to drag wounded or drowning comrades from the water and many who had somehow reached the beach safely the first time toppled dead across the bodies of the men they had returned to help.

There was no place to hide. By seven o'clock two thirds of Company A of the 116th Regiment were dead.

There were heroes at Omaha no one will ever know about because most of them are dead and the heroism of the others is known only to themselves. Brigadier General S. L. A. Marshall, the unexcelled army historian who, by his on-the-spot interviews in World War II, has done more than any other single man to preserve the truth about war in fact and spirit, says about this landing: "Disproportionate attention was paid to the little element of courageous success in a situation which was largely characterized by tragic failure."

Elements of the 1st Division's 16th Regiment coming in on Fox Green near the other end of the crescent-shaped beach were no better off than the men on Dog Green. Their 27 DD tanks were at the bottom somewhere out in the Channel behind them. German gun positions were set up here so that they shot across the beach. Their muzzle flashes were hidden from naval gunners scanning the shore by concrete walls only slightly less than parallel to the water. A handful of men who stayed in the surf, moving in with the tide, reached the base of the bluffs, but many of them were wounded and most of them had nothing to shoot with anyway.

A few brave men, or men who did not have the death fear, tried to get the others on their feet at isolated places along Omaha. Soldiers had been trained to believe that fewer of them would be killed if they were aggressive and kept moving up. But they knew this was true generally but not specifically. Few soldiers will be killed in a battle that is won quickly, but more of the ones who go forward to win it will die.

The engineer demolition men had not been able to open more than a dozen lanes through the mines and obstacles. All up and down the six miles of Omaha successive waves of assault troops met the same fate as the first wave. The shallow waters

off the beach were littered with smoking hulks of landing boats, landing ships, tanks, and dead and dying men. Small boats, moving in under fire, heard the plaintive cries of the wounded drowning and could not stop to help. The dukws had been overloaded with ammunition and artillery pieces. Dozens of them sank far out in the bay. Some were blown into the sky offshore, when they hit the teller mines set on the beach obstacles, and all but a handful of those that reached the beach were picked off by German artillery before they could get their wheels under them and move to any shelter.

Where tanks reached the beaches, their commanders were faced with a terrible decision. They could not stop because they would certainly be struck immediately by German shells and yet the beach was littered with dead and wounded Americans. The tank commanders had to give the order to keep rolling, and the thirty-ton M–4s rumbled over the dead and wounded, their tracks pressing each body as thin as a flower in a book.

Some of the engineers working in three or four feet of water demolishing obstacles, to clear paths for the boats coming in, were carrying fused blocks of TNT when they were hit. The blast parted the water in a crater that revealed the Channel bottom for an instant. The spume, flaked with blood and flesh, settled back into the water, and in the reports drawn up days later such a soldier was listed as "missing."

Infantrymen stopped long enough to pull a wounded comrade to a sitting position against a pole or concrete obstacle so that he would not be drowned when the tide moved in. The German machine-gunners on the bluffs, never sure these men were dead, poured bullets into the bodies until they dropped apart.

Losses (the communiqué from Allied Headquarters was to say later) ARE LESS THAN ANTICIPATED.

BEHIND THE WALL

When the first paratrooper dropped into Normandy, General Erwin Rommel was on his way back to Germany by car for a brief rest. He wished to be at home for his wife's birthday and he desperately wanted to talk to Hitler personally about problems concerning the Atlantic Wall. His meteorologist had given him the same weather report for the Channel that Stagg had given Eisenhower so it did not seem probable to Rommel that the attack would come in the few days he was away.

In Berchtesgaden, Adolf Hitler had gone to bed late.

In his headquarters near Paris, von Rundstedt got the first scattered reports of Allied paratroop landings. Through the night he got fragmentary communiqués that indicated no pattern. He did not know how many had landed and he did not know whether they would be followed by seaborne troops. At 2:15 A.M. Major General Max Pemsel at Seventh Army Headquarters reported to General Speidel, who was in charge of Rommel's Fifteenth Army headquarters during his absence:

> ENGINE NOISES ARE AUDIBLE FROM THE SEA COAST OF COTENTIN PENINSULA. SHIPS LOCATED BY RADAR OFF CHERBOURG. INDICATIONS OF LARGE-SCALE OPERATION.

For some reason von Rundstedt refused to believe this report, and within half an hour Speidel had sent an answer to Pemsel:

> C-IN-C, WEST, DOES NOT CONSIDER THIS TO BE A MAJOR OPERATION.

The Germans had little to go by. They had ninety radar stations in the area, but all of them had been accurately and repeatedly bombed by R.A.F. and Ninth Air Force planes, so that on the night of June 5–6 they were of little use. The Luftwaffe had been so badly beaten that it could provide no observation, and the Germans were reduced to relying on what they could see with their eyes and hear with their ears. As a result the great Invasion armada wasn't detected until it reached its staging area ten miles off the French coast.

Radar stations still operating in the Pas-de-Calais, however, which had been intentionally passed over by bombers, picked up and reported the approach in that direction of the Allied "dummy" fleet. Reports of paratroop landings came from places as remote as Le Havre and Rouen, and the Germans had no way of knowing that these were brought about by the firecracker dummies dropped in those areas. Whatever the situation, Hitler had told von Rundstedt that he was not to commit reserve divisions without permission. At 4 A.M. this permission was requested and promptly rejected. It is not clear whether Hitler rejected the request before he went to bed or whether Field Marshal Jodl declined to wake the Fuehrer and made the decision himself, believing it would also have been Hitler's.

Despite their lack of information, the Germans located the main paratroop drops as being around the mouth of the Orne River between Caen and the Channel and in the area around Ste.-Mère-Église. During the night the 21st Panzer Division was ordered to move to counterattack the British 6th at Caen east of the Orne and several units were ordered out against the United States paratroop concentrations.

When the seaborne landings began at dawn, the Germans were still waiting to see where they were going to be hit hardest. On Omaha, the crack 1st and 29th U.S. Divisions ran head-on into the experienced German 352nd Division, which had somehow moved into the Omaha sector during May without being reported by Allied Intelligence agents. This was the single most unfortunate circumstance of the Invasion for the Allies, and yet, like the bad weather and limited visibility which had lulled the Germans into a temporary sense of security, the early disaster at Omaha contributed to the Germans' defeat. At eight o'clock on the morning of D-Day a Wehrmacht officer in one of the 352nd's re-enforced concrete battle stations surveyed the inferno below him and finally made telephone contact with division headquarters. The greatest record-keepers of any war, the Germans kept a record, later captured, of this report:

THE ENEMY IS LOOKING FOR COVER AT THE EDGE OF THE WATER BEHIND COASTAL-ZONE OBSTACLES. A GREAT MANY MOTOR VEHICLES ARE BURNING ON THE BEACH. THE OBSTACLE DEMOLITION SQUADS HAVE ABANDONED THEIR ACTIVITIES. DEBARKATION FROM LANDING BOATS HAS CEASED. . . . THE FIRE

OF OUR BATTLE POSITIONS AND OUR ARTILLERY IS ACCURATE AND HAS INFLICTED MANY CASUALTIES ON THE ENEMY. THERE ARE MANY DEAD AND WOUNDED MEN ON THE BEACH.

It wasn't much, but it was enough to further confuse the German High Command about the Allied intent: Was this or was this not the main effort? Were the major landings still to be made on the Pas-de-Calais, after German reserves in that area had been sucked into countering this weak diversion in Normandy?

As late as 1:35 on D-Day the 352nd Division reported to army headquarters that the invasion on their front had been completely smashed and that there was no need to send reenforcements. They were apparently unaware of the magnitude of the Allied landings there, and almost ignorant of the tremendous forces following the United States 4th Division ashore on Utah Beach. As a result, the Germans concentrated their efforts against the building British forces near Caen. They planned to throw the 12th Panzer, the 21st Panzer and the Panzer Lehr Division into that front, but because of the situation brought about by Hitler's insistence that no moves be made without his permission, no decisive counterattack was mounted anywhere.

While the bloody battle raged on Omaha, the United States 4th Infantry Division was landing on Utah with little opposition. In many places the beach area was separated from the mainland of the Cotentin Peninsula by narrow strips of water or marshy areas. Several small groups of paratroopers had worked their way inland toward this water and, as retreating Germans raced across the causeways, they were cut down by men of the 82nd Airborne waiting for them on the other side.

Most of General Ridgway's chopped-up division was still inland and desperately in need of help. The 4th's first objective was to drive in and link up with these airborne troops. (The landings on Utah were so immediately successful and those on Omaha so disastrous that at one point during the morning General Omar Bradley, offshore on the heavy cruiser command ship *Augusta*, briefly considered shifting the landings of all following assault waves to Utah. The idea was abandoned as impractical.)

THE RANGERS

Between the hell of Omaha and the relative heaven of Utah, the 2nd and 5th Ranger Battalions fought for the high rock cliffs jutting into the Bay of the Seine. Every Ranger had been trained so that he could climb one hundred feet of rope with a fifty-pound pack on his back. Their objectives were the German gun positions on Pointe du Hoc and Pointe de la Percée to the right of Omaha. At H-hour minus 20, eighteen medium bombers of the Ninth Air Force hit Pointe du Hoc and the heavy guns of the battleship *Texas* kept pounding away until a few minutes before 6:30.

Pointe du Hoc itself was to be taken by three Ranger companies carried to the base of the cliff by ten British-manned LCAs. Each landing boat carried twenty men and was equipped with three rocket mounts for hurling rope and grapnel hooks over the top of the precipice. Four dukws were to follow the LCAs. The amphibious trucks were equipped with hundred-foot extension ladders. This was, on the surface at least, the most dangerous D-Day assignment.

Eight miles offshore, one LCA carrying Captain Harold Slater and twenty men swamped and sank. Nine boats pushed on. The shoreline was barely visible from the Channel because of the smoke of fires set on the bluffs by the bombardment, but as the nine boats neared land Colonel James E. Rudder realized they were headed not for Pointe du Hoc but for Pointe de la Percée, three miles east.

(The relationship between Army and Navy personnel, whether British or American, was not always amicable during the D-Day operation. The Navy men understandably wanted to drop their load as quickly as possible and get back out. The Army men on board wanted to be given every chance to live once they got off, regardless of the boat's safety. The ground forces were never satisfied with their air support. The paratroopers were highly critical, in many cases, of their transport pilots. The conflict did not even stop between services. For the most part no single fighting unit was ever quite happy about the help it was being given from the squad or the platoon or the division, or "the

British," on its flank. On D-Day there were several incidents of drawn pistols and fist fights between naval and ground force commanders on board the small landing craft.)

The navigational error meant that the nine boats had to proceed directly west now, close in to the beach and parallel to it, running the gauntlet of German fire from the bluffs. The landing party arrived at the base of Pointe du Hoc forty minutes behind schedule, and during the period between the bombardment's ceasing and the Rangers' starting up the cliffs, the Germans on top had time to recover. Fortunately for the Rangers, both the British destroyer *Talybont* and the United States *Satterlee* saw the error and opened fire again on German troops at the top.

The Germans, battered as they were, opened up with small arms fire as the Rangers touched down. As they raced for the base of the cliff about fifteen men were ripped with bullets from above, and, once they reached a point below the heights where they could not be reached by direct fire, the Germans started rolling fused hand grenades down the front of the cliff. In addition, the Germans had hung 200 mm shells on wires along the cliff so that they could be blown with a push of a button.

One by one and in small groups, the Rangers scaled the suicidal cliffs in the face of these enemy actions. Their ropes were cut from above, their grapnel hooks were dislodged in some cases, and the rocks that had been loosened by the bombardment caused frequent landslides. Yet about 120 of the 200 Rangers who attacked Pointe du Hoc reached the top, drove the Germans back and eliminated it as the single most dangerous enemy defensive position. The last stubborn enemy machine-gun pillbox, which the Rangers could not take, was chopped off the cliff and dropped into the water below by accurate artillery fire called in from the *Satterlee* by the Navy's shore fire control party that went in with Rudder's men.

BRITISH BEACHES

To the east along the coast, the British on Gold and Sword, separated by the Canadians on Juno, were faced with a different

problem. There were no sandy bluffs behind the beaches, but, instead, across the usual resort-town road running parallel with the beach, there were a series of small towns, vacation homes and hotels.

The British had, for more than a year, been sneaking two daring frogmen onto the beaches at night to take samples of the footing infantrymen and tanks might expect in specific beach areas. Two days before the Invasion two midget submarines, less than fifty feet long and five feet in diameter, had been dispatched to lie off the French coast. These two midget subs were to locate shore positions and act as guiding beacon lights for landing ships approaching in the darkness of early D-Day morning. Preceding the actual landing boats, one hundred and fifty British frogmen, who were also demolition experts, swam in to start blowing obstacles from the path of the oncoming Invasion force. British ingenuity and cunning were very apparent in OVERLORD planning, but when the time came it was the tough, well-trained British soldiers who made the landings a success.

On the whole British and Canadian landings were not as difficult as those on Omaha, although you could not have told that to the men in the second wave, who found several hundred of the East Yorkshire Regiment dead and dying on the beach near Ouistreham. Resistance on the British and Canadian beaches was spotty. The Hampshire Regiment spent eight hours taking out the rugged defenses in front of the town of Le Hamel and their losses were heavy, but immediately to their left men of the First Dorset Regiment had pushed inland within half an hour of landing. Again, on the beach to the right of Le Hamel there was so little opposition that the medical corpsmen had nothing to do but help unload ammunition.

The 3rd Canadian Division came in on either side of the mouth of the Seulles River and ran into serious trouble on the

The Rangers scale rocky Pointe du Hoc.

rocky reefs offshore. In one battalion, twenty of twenty-four land-ing craft were wrecked on the beach obstacles and on the reefs. Another landed by error in front of a heavily fortified German gun position and was held down for five hours until a United States destroyer moved to within a few hundred yards of the beach and blasted away at point-blank range.

The 50th Northumbrian Division and 8th Armored Brigade on the British westernmost flank had, by late evening, chopped out a piece of the French coast about six miles wide and six miles deep. They were astride the road from Caen to Bayeux, and this was important, because it was the main route over which the Germans might have moved forces to counterattack the Ameri-cans clinging by their fingernails to Omaha, seven miles west.

BY EVENING

The problem at Omaha had still not been solved by evening. While most German gun positions had been taken, there were still isolated machine-gun positions firing on the beaches and German artillery behind Carentan was hitting the coastline with regularity. There were only seven artillery pieces ashore and resupply and re-enforcement of the exhausted men were difficult because the beaches were cluttered with burned and burning ships, landing craft, tanks, dukws, and dead and dying men. Only two of the five exits from the beach were open. A haze of smoke hung low all along the six miles of sand.

Offshore, more than fifty tanks sat on the Channel bottom and most of their crews were still in them. One quartermaster unit lost all but thirteen of thirty-five two-and-a-half ton trucks to the sea; and the Navy, at Omaha alone, lost fifty landing craft and ten larger vessels. These figures are for destroyed, not damaged.

Inland a few small groups of exceptionally aggressive men had penetrated as deep as a mile and a half, and what was left of the 5th Rangers had joined with the remnants of the 1st and 2nd Battalions of the 116th Infantry to take Vierville. This force of about six hundred men was isolated from the rest of the beachhead. The main body occupied the narrow sector between the towns of St.-Laurent and Colleville, but no one had enough ammunition to do much more than hope the Germans would not counterattack in strength during the night.

On the happy beach, Utah, the 4th Infantry Division was almost intact and ready to fight. They had moved six miles inland to a point near the main road leading up the Peninsula to Cherbourg, and were in a position to drive across the narrow strip and cut off the German 91st Division stationed on the Cotentin. While reports from the 82nd Airborne indicated its position was shaky, Ridgway's men had occupied a lot of territory; and as soon as the 4th drove inland these United States islands could be linked, to provide a large consolidated foothold at the base of the peninsula.

There are no exact figures, because no one stood with a counter ticking off the invaders as they hit the beaches; but it has been estimated that by the end of the first twenty-four hours the Allies had about one hundred thousand men in France. Before the end of June, there would be nine hundred and eighty thousand.

By the end of D-Day Allied troops had not reached all their initial objectives, but they had punched a dozen holes in Hitler's Atlantic Wall and re-enforcements were pouring through those holes. The plug had been pulled from the vast reservoir of men and materials in the British Isles. Thousands of carriers moved between English ports and the French coast with the steady persistence of working ants.

To the east (or left going into France) the British had about sixty thousand men ashore and more than three hundred Churchill and Sherman tanks. They had pushed inland but were unable to take their primary objective, the destroyed French city of Caen. Caen was the hub of the German wheel, and despite the confusion of command which prevented an effective counterattack by them, their strong forces there could not be overrun by the British.

To their right, the Canadians on Juno had moved inland as

much as seven miles, although there still existed a dangerous four-mile gap between themselves and the Royal Marines on the western end of Sword. At about 9 P.M. General Edger Feuchtinger's 21st Panzer Division, with fifty tanks and a battalion of infantry, had almost reached the coast when the single largest glider-borne force of the day swept in and landed behind the Germans. The two hundred and fifty gliders carried infantrymen, small tanks, jeeps and artillery, and enough to fill the corridor. The Germans, unable to get re-enforcements because of Hitler's edict that he alone could commit the reserve divisions, were defeated in this single most dangerous D-Day probe.

In most of their beach areas, the fiercely proud Canadian soldiers pushed forward with relentless fighting efficiency. The two deepest penetrations by Allied forces on D-Day were made by the Canadian Royal Winnipeg Rifles and the Regina Rifles. Both these regiments moved two miles inland before noon.

Although the ground forces were under the overall command of Montgomery, his word carried more weight in the British sector subcommanded by General M. C. Dempsey than it did in the American sector under Bradley. At his insistence, the British Second Army went in with more armored support in front of them or next to them; and postwar arguments have been advanced that this was the reason for relatively light British casualties. The fact is that the British sector, with its sloping beach, was better suited for the movement of armor once it reached land. In some cases, on the United States beaches, tanks had no place to go once they got ashore and were caught by the flood tide up against the bluffs, unable to find any exit to the plateaus above them. The British, however, did use the flail tank, which the Americans had rejected, with considerable success, clearing paths through heavily mined fields behind the beaches.

Through the day the Allied Commanders had many pleasant and unpleasant surprises. Although they were appalled by the reports they were getting from Omaha, they knew before noon that the landings were going to stick and tension was eased on several counts.

First, the Germans had not resorted to using gas or bacteria. Although there had never been much talk about this, it was considered a possibility so likely that every man carried a gas mask and wore the uncomfortable anti-gas, impregnated clothing. The Allies were prepared to retaliate with gas on a large scale, but even with air dominance gas might have made the Invasion impossible.

The second pleasant surprise was the absence of the Luftwaffe. Except for one halfhearted and ineffectual attack by a few Junkers–88s on the British beaches, the Luftwaffe did not poke its nose in the air June 6. Barrage balloons lifted over the attack areas proved to be unnecessary, and when it was discovered that German artillery inland was using them as target markers and consequently doing some effective shelling on Sword, the balloons there were cut loose.

Third, and this was partially anticipated, the German Navy offered little opposition. Like the Luftwaffe, it had been largely defeated from the air long before D-Day. In Le Havre, Lieutenant Commander Heinrich Hoffman got word of the Invasion and set out to meet this fleet of more than five thousand ships with a flotilla of three tiny E-boats. In the only naval action of the day, Hoffman launched eighteen torpedoes and sent the Norwegian transport *Svenner* to the bottom with a direct hit amidships. Other than this one action, the naval forces' only worry was from German shore batteries and minefields. The United States destroyer *Corry,* doing effective work offshore at Utah, sank within minutes after it was all but cut in two by a mine detonated squarely under it.

D-Day was the beginning of the end for Adolf Hitler, and it was the last day of life for many British and American soldiers. With all the counting of things and the military shuffling of pieces of paper, no one seems to know how many. The United States First Army listed 1465 dead on D-Day. They listed 3184 wounded, but that doesn't mean much because the boy with four toes of his right foot blown off and the boy who still lies in a Veterans' hospital eating through a straw with his face gone are both

"wounded." They listed 1954 missing; but, after a while, all "missing" means is that they never found the body. British losses, officially unannounced, were comparable.

The best summary of D-Day, June 6, 1944, came from Joseph Stalin in a note addressed to Winston Churchill dated June 11:

THE HISTORY OF WAR DOES NOT SHOW ANY SUCH UNDER-TAKING SO BROAD IN CONCEPT, SO GRANDIOSE IN SCALE, SO MASTERLY IN EXECUTION.

THE BULGE

ON THE FIFTEENTH OF DECEMBER, 1944, Elizabeth Taylor opened in *National Velvet* at the Radio City Music Hall in New York, skiing conditions were reported "excellent" at Lake Placid, and the tobacco companies were trying to persuade the Federal Government that they should be declared an "essential industry" so that they could increase their cigarette production by one third to satisfy the demand.

In Europe Allied soldiers were advancing on Germany along an unbroken line six hundred miles long reaching from Switzerland to the English Channel. Elements of the United States First and Ninth Armies were across the Roer River in strength. In the north British Field Marshal Bernard Montgomery was demanding that he be allowed to shoot straight for Berlin, and in the south General George S. Patton was claiming that nothing was holding back his Third Army in the Saar except red tape and lack of gas for his tanks. Supreme Headquarters issued a proclamation stating that, as Allied troops overran the Wehrmacht, all stolen art found in Germany would be returned to its rightful owners; and at his headquarters, outside Paris, General Dwight D. Eisenhower had not given up his hope for victory by Christmas.

At 5:40 in the foggy morning of December 16, two thousand German artillery pieces started bombarding the thinnest sector of the American line to open a path through the difficult, snow-covered Ardennes Forest for a quarter of a million of Hitler's soldiers and twenty-three hundred tanks. It was the beginning of the last great German offensive and the end of Allied dreams of an easy victory.

Before it stopped there were eighty thousand American casualties. The Germans lost many more than that.

"There is no doubt," Eisenhower said, "the Ardennes was one of the greatest killing grounds of the war."

AFTER THE DAY

ON JULY 25, 1944, a month and a half after the D-Day landings in Normandy, American forces had finally punched a clean hole through the tough crust of German resistance in France. General

Patton's Third Army was shoved through the hole opened at Saint-Lô by the heavy-duty First Army, and started to move. Field Marshal Bernard Montgomery had not been able to break out with his British forces at Caen; one of the postwar arguments among military strategists is whether Montgomery was militarily inept or whether his forces were actually making it easier for the United States advance by engaging the heaviest elements of the German force there. Whatever the case, Montgomery was aware of the criticism at the time and it influenced his actions through the rest of the war.

The fight across France was a series of Allied successes. The Germans stood and fought where they could; they made every victory difficult; but they were being overwhelmed, and the Allies usually had some tactical choice. As they approached Paris, late in August, Eisenhower sidestepped the issue of whether the British or the Americans should free that city by giving the job to the French 2nd Division Blindée. Paris was lightly defended and was of more psychological than strategical importance.

While blatant elements of the British press were demanding that Monty, their hero of El Alamein, be given a more important role in the Allied advance, and while headline-conscious elements of the American press were giving their play to Patton's end run, General Courtney Hodges's powerful First Army was doing the lion's share of the fighting. It was Eisenhower's basic plan to advance into Germany in one long, strong wave rather than to drive one column deep. General Omar Bradley was commander of the 12th Army Group, the intermediary headquarters between Eisenhower and the three United States armies eventually committed: the First, Third and General William Simpson's Ninth. Montgomery commanded all British forces.

One of Eisenhower's headaches was the result of the personalities of his subordinates. They made it difficult for him to maintain his tactical plan. Bradley, the American, was close to the quiet, reserved caricature of the British general seen in American papers. Montgomery, on the other hand, had many of the characteristics of the British image of the cocky, loud-mouthed American. Patton had them too, and while Bradley was nominally his boss, it had not always been that way and Bradley had a hard time forgetting it: until Patton slapped the battle-sick soldier in a hospital in North Africa, he had been Bradley's senior in command. Both Montgomery and Patton wanted to go win the war by themselves. There was little doubt of their military competence in certain circumstances, and either might conceivably have accomplished a quick victory; but that was not the war the methodical Eisenhower had planned. If he had assigned additional manpower and supplies to either it would have been at the expense of the rest.

Patton bragged of stealing supplies and gas from First Army dumps to sustain his drive in the Saar to the south, and insistently pushed farther forward than was good for the rest of the Allied line. Montgomery, to the north, was so confident that he could reach Berlin quickly if given some of Bradley's manpower that he flew to Eisenhower and, face to face, made a strongly worded demand.

The few senior officers present at that meeting became increasingly uneasy as Montgomery's voice rose while he sat opposite the Supreme Allied Commander. Eisenhower was slow to anger, but Montgomery was treading on dangerous ground. Once angered, Eisenhower struck with incisiveness against the object of his displeasure, and associates knew this might be the end of what had never been a really beautiful friendship.

As those in the room waited for Eisenhower's slow-burning fuse to reach the explosives, he is reported to have reached out his hand and placed it on Montgomery's knee.

"Steady, Monty," Eisenhower said. "You can't talk to me like that. I'm your boss."

Montgomery is said to have risen to the occasion by pausing for an instant and then saying quickly, "I'm sorry, Ike."

Montgomery proceeded to expose his plan to leave the Allied front behind and, with added strength taken from it, push quickly on past the Ruhr and into Berlin. If this had been accomplished, it would have a great British victory, and it has been suggested that the plan was denied because of political considerations. In the light of all the facts, it seems highly unlikely that Eisenhower

ever gave such considerations more thought than diplomacy required of him.

The plan for the broad advance into Germany that left no
stone of resistance unturned called for massive numbers of men,
equipment and resupply. The Allies were still using the man-
made harbors at the Normandy beaches, and Cherbourg was
cleared for docking. The British had taken Antwerp intact, and
this was a major help, but the stubborn fact remained that as
Allied forces pushed on, the advance demanded more men and
supply lines became longer. Inversely, German lines were becoming shorter, and as their armies were compressed into the Fatherland from the east by the Russians and from the west by the
Allies, this nut became harder to crack.

By the middle of September, as the Allies came up against
the border rivers and the Siegfried Line, Hitler's West Wall, the
advance slowed perceptibly. The German defensive position,
unlike the fortresslike French Maginot Line, was made up of a
series of effective strongpoints and pillboxes covering each other
and all likely approach points.

Inside his constricted empire, Adolf Hitler looked anxiously
at the large noose tightening around his neck and searched desperately for a weak point where he could break it. For a variety
of reasons, he chose the Allied western front. He believed the
British were overextended in their war effort and could summon
up little in the way of reserves in the event of a counterattack.
He did not hold American forces in high regard, and he further
felt that they had less interest in the war and would respond
less tenaciously to a counterthrust than had the fanatical Russians fighting for their homeland.

Once Hitler had decided his last-gasp fight would be a drive
to the west, selection of the specific battleground was not difficult.
The American sector of the six-hundred-mile front between
Aachen and Metz lay in the frostbitten Ardennes, the difficult
forested mountain region through which his forces had driven
into France against the British and French in 1940. This area was
lightly held by the Allies. They were thinking primarily of the
offensive, and they had planned none in this area. The thin Ameri-

can lines were manned here by two types of units: battle-weary divisions which had been sent there to rest and recuperate while their weakened forces were built up, and green troops which had never been shot at.

In the light of history, Hitler's Ardennes offensive seems to have been destined for failure and those of his staff officers who lived to write about it after the war have assured the world that they disapproved of it at the time. Under the circumstances in which Hitler found himself, however, it was probably the best long-shot gamble that he could have taken. The lesser measures advocated *ex post facto* by German officers might have been more successful, but a limited success would not have saved Germany at that point.

Hitler drew the outline of the bold plan and his most trusted lieutenant, General Alfred Jodl, filled in the details. Field Marshal Gerd von Rundstedt, once relieved of command of the German western front, was placed in overall charge of the operation, deceptively code-named WACHT AM RHEIN. Under von Rundstedt, Field Marshal Walter Model directed thirty-two strong divisions divided among three German armies. The fanatical Nazi General Sepp Dietrich was in command of the crack Sixth SS Panzer Army. The Fifth Panzer was under the armored genius General Hasso von Manteuffel. The Seventh Army was given to steady Wehrmacht old-timer General Erich Brandenberger.

Brandenberger was to drive into the gap and swing south to hold off Patton's army, which they knew would be brought north when the Allies realized the scale of the counteroffensive. The two panzer armies, with new tanks reserved for this occasion, were to smash through the opening in the Allied lines, race sixty miles to the Meuse River and then cut northwest and retake the vital port at Antwerp, one hundred and twenty-five miles away.

"It was a desperate gamble," Jodl said after the war, "but we were in a desperate situation, and the only chance to save it was by a desperate decision. We had to stake everything."

Von Rundstedt, echoing the statements of millions of Germans at lesser levels who made lesser decisions, said after the war that he had little to do with the attack.

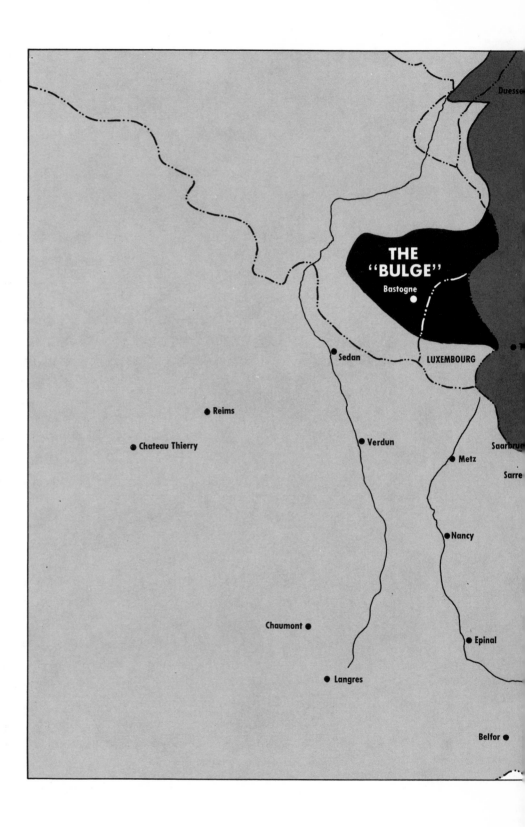

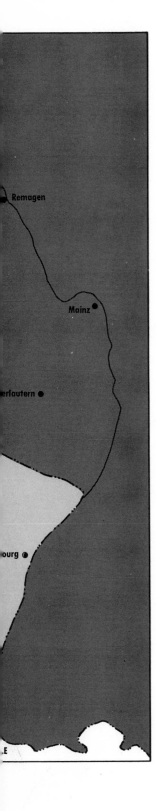

Remagen

Mainz

erlautern ●

ourg ●

E

"I strongly object to the fact that this stupid operation in the Ardennes is sometimes referred to as 'the Rundstedt Offensive.' I had nothing to do with it. It came to me as an order complete to the last detail. . . . It was only up to me to obey."

There is evidence that von Rundstedt did actually express his disapproval of the scope of the offensive at the time, but Hitler understood better than any of his generals that this was the time for an all-or-nothing counterattack.

"I am determined to carry out this operation despite all the risks," Hitler said. "Even if the impending Allied attacks on either side of Metz and toward the Ruhr should result in great loss of territory, I am determined, nevertheless, to go ahead with this attack."

Ready critics of Hitler's military ability should remember that he was not concerned with winning a battle. He was out to conquer the world. What he needed most for this in December 1944 was time. German scientists were improving the V–1 flying bomb and had completed the rocket-propelled V–2s. Hitler also knew his scientists were not far from producing an atom bomb. If he could hold off the Russians and the Allies for another six months, he knew the whole course of the war might be changed. His best hope for this was to retake Antwerp, cut off Allied troops north of Belgium and drive a wedge between the rest of the Allied troops on the Continent and their supply lines.

On December 12, four days before the great offensive, Hitler called together all the senior officers who were to take part. With his talent for convincing anyone in his presence that the moon was made of green cheese, Hitler infused many of them who came there full of doubts with his own apparent optimism. He was convinced, or at least made it appear so, that Antwerp could be taken. Careful weather reports from meteorologists on U-boats in the North Atlantic had assured him of the bad weather paradoxically necessary for the German thrust. It was imperative that the offensive be shielded from Allied air attack by close to zero visibility. And where would they get gas enough? Hitler triumphantly announced that his panzer legions would stop for gas supplies at the best and closest locations—the American gas dumps they would be overrunning shortly after the attack shoved off.

Without air reconnaissance, the Germans did not know where the American supply dumps were; Hitler was simply confident there must be many of them. (He had no way of knowing that, earlier in December, Bradley had given Eisenhower one reassuring bit of information when the Supreme Commander noted with some anxiety that the Ardennes sector was very lightly held. Bradley admitted to Eisenhower that his line was thin there, but added that he had been careful not to place any major supply installations in the area between the Meuse and the Ardennes.)

With spotty Intelligence information and limited air reconnaissance, Bradley was not fully aware of German troop movements to the Schnee Eifel area of the Ardennes, but he had been given some indication of a buildup there. It was, however, the considered opinion of his Intelligence staff that von Rundstedt would never commit major elements of his reserve to an attack in that area, when it had no chance for anything more than limited success. Bradley knew von Rundstedt well, but, in trying to anticipate German moves with military logic, the Allies neglected to consider that they were trying to outthink someone who was not thinking rationally: Adolf Hitler.

THE AWFUL SURPRISE

With the exception of the garrison at Pearl Harbor, no American force was ever taken more by surprise than were the troops hit by the full force of the German blow in the Ardennes. Along a seventy-mile front, between Monschau and Echternach, thirty-one German divisions smashed their way into three United States infantry divisions—the 4th, 28th and 106th—and one armored division, the 9th. On the Our River front, the 28th Division, defending a line thirty miles long, was overpowered by five German divisions.

To the south, the experienced 4th Infantry Division held their ground fairly well. The first and greatest American tragedy of the Battle of the Bulge was the 106th. No United States division ever suffered such catastrophic losses in such a short time. Within forty-eight hours two of this division's three regiments had been surrounded and slaughtered. The only men who lived, or were not captured, fled in terror. By December 22, the 106th was a broken unit, without men or command, having lost more than 70 per cent of its combat personnel.

The story of the 106th is unique in battle. On December 11, 1944, the 106th took over the defense of the St.-Vith area from the battle-seasoned 2nd Division. The 2nd had been in the Ardennes to recuperate; the 106th was being sent there for different reasons. This division, with the highest numerical designation in the United States Army, had the lowest average age. It had been assigned the first eighteen-year-old draftees, and the average age of the division was just twenty-two. None of them had ever heard a shot fired by an enemy. They needed seasoning badly, and the relatively quiet Ardennes seemed to Allied commanders to be the best place for it.

If a soldier lives for a month in battle, his chances of living the second month are greatly improved. A man who has been exposed to enemy fire knows the sounds and sights of war. The sounds, especially, are important. A veteran infantryman can distinguish between perhaps twenty-five small-arms pieces. From the sound he knows what gun it is, how far away and who is firing it. He knows a dozen artillery pieces and what types of shells are being fired by them. He knows when to duck and when not to bother. He knows when to fire and when to sit tight. Most of all, a veteran infantryman gets to know when there is cause for alarm and when there is not.

The old hand at this time could watch a wave of green-clad German infantrymen surge forward and quietly let it approach to within a few hundred yards before calling for mortar fire from the gun crew behind him. Panic was the nemesis of green troops, and many men of the 106th panicked. They were no less brave than the men of the great 1st Division, but they did not know how to fight; as a result they were virtually wiped out by the three Volksgrenadier divisions and the one panzer division that ripped into them on the morning of December 16.

In January, Secretary of War Henry L. Stimson gave some indication of what had happened to the 106th. It was announced by his office in Washington that, during the Battle of the Bulge, 416 men of that division were known killed, 1246 were wounded and 7001 were ominously "missing in action."

Surviving members of the 106th were subject to strong criticism by other units up and down the line, and many of the men tore their "roaring lion" shoulder patches from their uniforms to keep from being identified with the ill-fated division. Other conscientious battle casualties among them wept at the thought that they had let down the rest of the United States Army. For all these green troops knew, war was always like that and no other division had ever turned and run. The men had no way of knowing that they had just taken the full force, head on, of the single strongest German attack of the war.

"No troops in the world," General Courtney Hodges said afterward, "disposed as your division was, could have withstood the impact of the German attack."

CONFUSION AND MASSACRE

Of the three combat regiments of the 106th, only the 424th lived to fight for St.-Vith, the important road center they were charged with guarding. The 423rd was lost by the end of the second day of the attack; the last word from the beleaguered 422nd came on December 19—a simple radio message: SEND US AMMUNITION.

The 424th managed to fall back into the town of St.-Vith with the German panzer division hard on its heels. Fortunately for the now disorganized regiment, Combat Command B of the 9th Armored Division advanced into the back end of town as the 424th retreated into the front end. They met in the middle.

"It was like a movie horse-opera," General Alan W. Jones, division commander of the 106th, said. "Tanks of the 9th Armored wheeled into position in the square just as the Tigers following us came over the brow of the hill to the east."

While the defense of the important road junction of St.-Vith eventually failed, the 106th salvaged some honor for the division by holding on by their teeth, with elements of the 7th and 9th Armored Division, for five long hard days. Quick capture of St.-Vith and of Bastogne, twenty miles to the west, was essential to the success of the German offensive. Between them, these towns commanded the only two north–south roads good enough for mass tank movements, and each was the hub through which passed five other important roads. There were only thirteen major roads running through the whole of the mountain area, and the Ardennes was necessarily a battle of roads. In many places the snow was waist-deep by late December and even without snow the tanks could not operate off the roads through the heavily forested mountain region.

Although the story of the collapse of the 106th was the one that spread through Allied lines, the veteran 28th Division didn't fare much better. Unlike the 106th, the 28th knew how to fight; but on the morning of December 16 the Germans struck with two full-strength panzer divisions, three infantry divisions, and one elite paratroop division. Two German divisions were assigned to each American regiment; the 28th Division was overwhelmed.

The Germans counted on confusing the Allied command with their surprise attack and in this they were not disappointed. No one at Bradley's 12th Army Group Headquarters knew exactly what had happened or where. It was first thought that the German attack was nothing more than a minor "spoiling action" designed to take some of the pressure off German troops defending positions near the Roer River and to the south in the Saar Basin. Bradley was talking with Eisenhower at Supreme Headquarters back near Paris when word of the German offensive first reached him. Neither man was aware of the full extent of the operation, but the order went out for the 7th Armored Division to move south from its position with the Ninth Army while the 10th Armored, attached to the Third Army, was to move north towards the Ardennes. This was a bucket of water on a forest fire, and it was two days later before the gravity of the situation was appreciated by the Allied Command.

The 7th Armored got its order to move out of its rest area

near Aachen late in the day of December 16. Before dawn the next morning General R. W. Hasbrouck had his division on the road headed laterally toward St.-Vith, fifty miles away. Twice during the day the division had to loop back west to avoid advance units of the 1st SS Panzer Division, which had made deep penetrations in the area. In its dash for St.-Vith, Hasbrouck's 7th Armored encountered an ebb tide of retreating service troops and disorganized infantrymen fleeing in the face of the terrifying German panzer thrust. One unit, the 285th Field Artillery Regiment, moved into the march column of the 7th Armored and was trapped by one lunging battalion of the SS division commanded by the ruthless SS colonel, Joachim Peiper.

These hardheaded young Nazis were triumphant with their quick successes of the day. They had been ordered, if they needed orders, to stage a *rabatz* against the Americans. *Rabatz* was the SS term for a terror-producing orgy of cruelty. Their only thought was to advance. They wanted no part of the problem of guarding prisoners. There is evidence that SS men equipped with pistols strode through the field kicking fallen men in the testicles and, where there was any reaction, the *coup de grâce* was given with a pistol shot through the head. The thing was nevertheless done hastily, and fifteen Americans lived to report the story.

(Years later von Rundstedt claimed that he first heard reports of the atrocity over the British Broadcasting Company radio and immediately demanded an explanation from Peiper. Peiper stated that the Americans had been taken prisoner by another unit and were being marched to the rear by a small number of German guards when they met the SS troopers. The SS men, Peiper claimed, thought they had encountered an American pocket of resistance and opened fire on them. He bolstered his story by claiming that the German guards were also killed.)

All along the sector United States troops had been overwhelmed or infiltrated, and for two days there was no front or rear to the line. Reports of the "Malmedy Massacre" and rumors of the work of Colonel Otto Skorzeny's 150th (Trojan Horse) Brigade added to the chaos. Skorzeny, Hitler's daring operative who had freed the imprisoned Mussolini, had under his command a small, hand-picked band of Germans trained to look and behave like Americans. They traveled in captured United States jeeps, Sherman tanks and General Motors trucks. Their mission was to drive through a hole near Stavelot and push quickly forward to the Meuse River, under the pretense of being a retreating United States unit. Their accomplishments were slight, but revelation of their existence, through radioed warnings to all American troops to be on the lookout for Germans posing as GIs, created havoc. No one trusted anyone whose face was not familiar, and Skorzeny was reported seen in several hundred places, including Paris. One rumor was that Skorzeny and a task force of about sixty men were headed for the Café de la Paix in Paris, where they were to join forces with some German sympathizers among the French and proceed to assassinate Eisenhower. A few hundred German paratroopers were actually dropped immediately behind Allied lines in Belgium; and, when this report was broadcast, everyone began to look like a German paratrooper in an American uniform to many Frenchmen and some excitable Allied personnel. One dead-serious message came into Allied Headquarters reporting that large numbers of paratroopers wearing nuns' habits had landed in one area. The Skorzeny rumors provided the only humor in an otherwise tragic situation. GI sentries up and down the line and back to Channel ports were demanding more proof of identity than the password of the day. If the guard happened to be from Iowa, he would demand that the soldier he was challenging prove his 100 per cent Americanism by naming the capital of that state. This led to all sorts of confusion, because half the time a soldier from the Bronx had gone to war thinking Omaha was a state. General Bradley was stopped frequently by sentries anxious to prove they were carrying out his security orders; he passed on questions such as how many home runs Babe Ruth had hit, but failed on one occasion when asked to name Betty Grable's third husband. Harry James was a little out of Bradley's line.

At the precise time Otto Skorzeny was being reported in several dozen places behind Allied lines, he was actually sitting in the Army headquarters of the relentless Sepp Dietrich. Dietrich's panzer forces had pushed far forward, but had not achieved the complete breakthrough they had hoped for. Skorzeny needed a gap through which he could push his largest units in order to race for the Meuse. Both Skorzeny and Dietrich considered the bold operation of the 150th Brigade a failure and Skorzeny reluctantly agreed to attach his forces to conventional German units.

What Skorzeny didn't know was that seven jeeploads of his "American" infiltrators were actually doing most effective work behind Allied lines. One team tore up the main telephone cable connecting Bradley with Hodges's First Army headquarters; a second team, stopped by an advancing American relief column, posed as retreating GIs and gave such a convincing account of the strength of the German forces "chasing" them that the whole relief column reversed its direction. Paradoxically, the greatest damage to the Allies was done by the one Skorzeny team they captured. These men revealed the plot, told how they had been schooled to smoke American cigarettes American-style, and tutored in dated American slang. This single report was the basis for all the rumors, and the prisoners did more damage by confessing their scheme than they ever could have done had they not been caught.

THE MERRY TROOPERS

By midmorning of December 17, Eisenhower and Bradley knew what their front-line commanders had known for almost twenty-four hours: this was no small-scale German attack. They reviewed their forces, looking for help. Back in Reims the rough, tough 82nd and 101st Airborne Divisions were doing what they did next best to fighting. Relieved after months in the line, they were rollicking in the streets and in the bistros with French women, singing, stealing, fighting among themselves and with French townspeople. Americans at home who thought GIs spent all their free time writing *Dear Mom* letters would have been appalled at the behavior of many of these soldiers. With guns at their sides and a path of conquest behind them, they were free of the restraints of normal society. They were eating, drinking and

making merry with any woman they could find because yesterday they had seen too many of their companions die.

The order went out and within ten hours these outfits had been pulled from every conceivable den in the area and put on the road to the front.

"Where do you want them?" Bradley asked Hodges when he finally reached him by phone.

"I need one at Bastogne and the other at Werbomont," Hodges said, "and the sooner the better."

To the south Patton was still sulking over having lost his 10th Armored when it was ordered to swing towards Ardennes shortly after the first German attack. He had no idea that this was only the start of what his Third Army would be asked to do.

The defense of St.-Vith was bolstered by the arrival of the 7th Armored Division, whose command pulled together parts of the 9th Armored and broken bits and pieces of the 106th. The German wave parted on this rock of resistance and flowed past it on either side but could not immediately take the vital rail and road hub. Although the Allies hardly realized it at the time, and although St.-Vith did fall on December 23, this was the beginning of the defeat of the German offensive.

South of St.-Vith, Manteuffel drove his Fifth Panzer Army for Houffalize and Bastogne. There was nothing much in his way except remnants of defeated and retreating United States troops; and General Heinrich von Luttwitz, given the job of taking Bastogne, did not anticipate any great problem. In Bastogne itself at this time, there was little else but General Troy Middleton's VIIIth Corps Headquarters and stragglers from General Dutch Cota's courageous but overwhelmed 28th Division. Middleton had no orders to hold Bastogne, and he had received no word that help was on the way. Actually, three forces were converging on that town as Middleton sat wondering what move to make.

By midnight of the eighteenth, von Luttwitz was within eight miles of the city and meeting only sporadic resistance.

"Take Bastogne at all costs," Manteuffel had told him, "otherwise it will remain an abscess in our line of communication."

The race to Bastogne among the 101st Airborne, the 10th Armored and von Luttwitz's three divisions was won in a photo finish by elements of the 10th Armored. Middleton immediately ordered them to keep going through the town, fan out and establish roadblocks when they met the advancing German columns. But less than one third of the 10th Armored had arrived, and they could not hold off the German surge. Enveloping Bastogne from three sides, the Germans came on. Racing through the night, the 101st drove for the last opening in the bag and got through before the Germans drew the string. Bastogne was surrounded, but the 101st's timely arrival had saved the 10th Armored from destruction—and now what? It appeared as if the 10th would later be destroyed, in company with the "Screaming Eagles" of the 101st.

The Germans now pressed in on Bastogne from all sides. It was bitter cold, and American forces were short of food and ammunition. Water froze in their canteens and the attack was so incessant that sleep was out of the question. The equipment-proud United States Army was somehow ill-equipped here for war in the snow, and GIs facing Germans in warm, white snowsuits improvised their own by pulling "tattletale gray" suits of long underwear over olive-drab battledress.

By the morning of December 22, the men in Bastogne were desperate. Under General Anthony McAuliffe, deputy commander of the 101st, they were resisting all around the perimeter, but losses in dead and wounded were high and, with no hope in sight, morale of the men started to dip.

Men of the 101st Airborne and the 10th Armored made strange bedfellows. Infantrymen look on a tank as a private fortress, heavily armored and mobile. They invariably think that it is the job of the tanks to move out in front of the infantry. Tank

A second enemy, snow, begins to fall
on the fields outside Bastogne.

corpsmen seldom see it that way. To them, a tank is a gas-and-explosive-laden trap, always a potential torch. To them, infantry-men are the probing fingers that move out and explore the points of resistance before the armor moves up to eliminate them.

In Bastogne, however, the 10th and the 101st worked to-gether. One tank-infantry patrol, probing the road towards Wiltz on the morning of the twenty-second, encountered two German tanks dug deep in the snow, being used as artillery pillboxes. The crew of one of the three Sherman tanks temporarily aban-doned the American vehicle and, in attempting to work around to the side of the German gun positions as infantrymen, became separated from the small party and could not get back to their tank, parked in a relatively safe position behind a stone farm-house. As the other two tank crews turned back to town, an Airborne sergeant and four of his men climbed up the sides of this deserted tank and started to drop down inside.

"Go ahead," the sergeant yelled to the astonished tankers, "we'll learn how to run the son-of-a-bitch, and follow you."

Before the Neufchâteau road was cut, isolating Bastogne, the 101st and 9th Armored were fighting as separate units with little co-operation. General McAuliffe, realizing that things would never work out this way, asked his corps commander, General Middleton, to assign the armored combat to him.

Colonel William L. Roberts of the armored unit objected strongly. "What do you know about using armor?" he demanded of McAuliffe.

"Perhaps," McAuliffe snapped back, "you'd like all of the 101st Division attached to *your* combat command."

Middleton settled the argument by phone after the last road out of Bastogne was cut on December 20. He put McAuliffe in overall command of the bastion. Thereafter, Colonel Roberts and McAuliffe worked efficiently together in harmony, and Roberts conducted what amounted to a school for infantry officers in the proper use of armor in battle.

As always, the Germans around Bastogne were doing things precisely. At precisely 11:30 on the morning of December 22, their bombardment stopped, rifle fire ceased, and four Germans carrying a white flag came up the road from Remoifosse. They were met by Sergeant Carl Dickinson, Sergeant Oswald Butler and Private Ernest Premetz. Premetz, a medic, spoke some German; and the German captain, accompanying the major in charge of the party, spoke English. The men took the Germans to Lieutenant Leslie Smith, leader of a weapons platoon. Smith blindfolded the two officers, left the two German enlisted men at his command post, and started for company headquarters. A series of phone messages brought Major Alvin Jones, who took the paper brought by the German major and read it:

TO THE U.S.A. COMMANDER OF THE ENCIRCLED TOWN OF BASTOGNE:

THE FORTUNE OF WAR IS CHANGING. THIS TIME THE U.S.A. FORCES IN AND NEAR BASTOGNE HAVE BEEN ENCIRCLED BY STRONG GERMAN ARMORED UNITS. MORE GERMAN ARMORED UNITS HAVE CROSSED THE RIVER OUR, NEAR ORTHEUVILLE, HAVE TAKEN MARCHE AND REACHED ST.-HUBERT BY PASSING THROUGH HOMORES-SIBRET-TILLET. LIBRIMONT IS IN GERMAN HANDS.

THERE IS ONLY ONE POSSIBILITY OF SAVING THE ENCIRCLED U.S.A. TROOPS FROM TOTAL ANNIHILATION: THAT IS THE HONORABLE SURRENDER OF THE ENCIRCLED TOWN. IN ORDER TO THINK IT OVER, A PERIOD OF TWO HOURS WILL BE GRANTED, BEGINNING WITH THE PRESENTATION OF THIS NOTE.

IF THIS PROPOSAL SHOULD BE REJECTED, ONE GERMAN ARTILLERY CORPS AND SIX HEAVY ANTIAIRCRAFT BATTALIONS ARE READY TO ANNIHILATE THE U.S.A. TROOPS IN AND NEAR BASTOGNE. THE ORDER FOR FIRING WILL BE GIVEN IMMEDIATELY AFTER THIS TWO-HOUR PERIOD.

ALL THE SERIOUS CIVILIAN LOSSES CAUSED BY THIS ARTILLERY FIRE WOULD NOT CORRESPOND WITH THE WELL-KNOWN AMERICAN HUMANITY.

THE GERMAN COMMANDER:
GENERAL VON LUTTWITZ, G.O.C.
XLVII PANZER CORPS

During the time it took to get the German officers to McAuliffe a rumor had spread all over Bastogne: four Germans had just come into town with a white flag. The Krauts were ready to give up.

This rumor suggested the attitude of the whole Bastogne contingent, and General McAuliffe shared the feeling. The answer he gave has been widely misinterpreted as the defiant epithet of a man willing to die before quitting. The Bastogne garrison, despite its losses, was far from defeatist, and when McAuliffe was told what was on the paper, his comment to the small gathering of officers was a light "Aw, nuts!"

McAuliffe sat down at the kitchen table in his headquarters to write a formal reply to the German surrender demand. With pencil poised, he looked around at his small staff and said: "I don't know what to tell them. What do I say?"

Behind him, Colonel H. W. O. Kinnard, his operations officer, said quietly, "That first remark of yours would be hard to beat."

McAuliffe couldn't recall what he'd said.

"You said 'Nuts,' " Kinnard told him.

Everyone in the room laughed and agreed it would be a fitting reply to the pompous German surrender ultimatum.

Colonel Joseph Harper, commander of the 327th Glider Infantry Regiment, into whose area the Germans had marched with the white flag, said he'd enjoy delivering the message.

Harper returned to where the German major and the captain were waiting.

"I have the American commander's reply," Harper said stiffly.

"Is it written?" the German captain asked.

"It is written," Harper said.

Harper handed the one-word message to the German captain. His blindfold was removed and he stared down at the piece of paper in his hand.

The captain gave the major what he thought was the translation of the word "Nuts."

"Well," said the major in German, "is that negative or affirmative?"

"Tell him," Harper said to the captain, "that 'Nuts' means

the same thing in English as 'Go to hell.' See if he understands that."

The Germans were led back to the road where they had first appeared.

"I'll tell you something else," Colonel Harper said as a parting shot. "If you continue to attack we'll kill every goddam German that tries to break into this city."

With that the four-man German surrender party was sent back down the road, the major grasping in his hand the war's most deathless message.

A ROCK OF RESISTANCE

During the rest of that day and night, things began to look worse for the men trapped at Bastogne. The three battalions of artillery had less than ten rounds of ammunition per gun; McAuliffe issued an order that the guns were not to be fired until the Germans surged forward *en masse*. On the roads circling the city, frustrated artillery gunners watched helplessly as columns of German panzers shuffled past like metal ducks in a shooting gallery.

Ammunition was not the only shortage. The men in the shallow holes in the fields around Bastogne lived on the ragged edge of freezing to death at night. The temperature reached thirteen degrees; the men were constantly cold, and hungry. One large store of flour was found in a civilian warehouse in town along with about four hundred pounds of coffee, and these supplies were distributed. Civilian homes in Bastogne were ransacked for blankets and sheets. The sheets were useful both for added warmth and as camouflage against the new-fallen snow.

Bastogne stands as a great example of what can be accomplished in wartime by men who keep their wits about them. The Bastogne garrison was in a continuous state of siege but they knew what they were doing and at no time was there panic. The 101st Airborne was accustomed to being surrounded in battle. They were inventive, tough and knowledgeable in all the tricks of war—but without food or ammunition things nevertheless

looked black. The Germans were blasting at them with the heavy artillery pieces they had jackknifed through the mountain passes. The night of the twenty-second an air-supply drop scheduled for 10 P.M. was canceled because of bad weather, and McAuliffe's confident "Nuts" had been based to a large extent on his belief that he would get relief from the air. Shortly after the word came that the transports could not drop the supplies, Hermann Goering's Luftwaffe made its first appearance in strength in months. When the bombs fell on "the Battered Bastards of Bastogne," as they were now calling themselves, it gave the Bastogne encirclement every dimension: in a two-and-a-half-mile ring around them were German infantrymen, tanks and artillery; below them was the cruelly hard, bitterly cold, snow-covered ground; and now, from above, bombs.

Everyone asked the natural question: "If the Luftwaffe can drop bombs, why in hell can't our Air Force drop supplies?"

It was apparent that the Germans were building up all around the perimeter for a major push into the city. Even small-arms ammunition was scarce now, and bravery alone was not enough to withstand a sustained attack. At 3:30 word reached headquarters that the 4th Armored Division was moving full speed toward Bastogne, to the aid of the two trapped divisions; but if the Germans launched their infantry and tank charge before the end of the day, the 4th Armored Division might arrive too late.

Although the Germans kept pounding away, there did not appear to be any immediate increase in the intensity of the bombardment after the rejection by McAuliffe of their surrender ultimatum. During the morning of December 23, word spread through the garrison that transport planes were on the way again; and this time the men were not disappointed. During the day two hundred and forty-one C–47s parachuted fifteen hundred loads of supplies to them. The drop was accurate and very successful. The tired, hungry men recovered 95 per cent of the supplies dropped—almost one hundred and fifty tons. Trucks and jeeps, often under direct fire from German artillery, scurried across the area distributing the supplies, and artillery guns had the first shells in the air again while others were still floating down by parachute.

This was only a stopgap aid, but more help was coming.

On the nineteenth of December, Eisenhower had met with Bradley, Patton and a representative from First Army (Hodges himself was just too busy to come).

"The present situation," Eisenhower said as the meeting started, "is to be regarded as one of opportunity for us and not of disaster. There will be only cheerful faces at this conference table."

"Yeah," said Patton enthusiastically, "let the bastards go all the way to Paris, then we'll cut 'em off and chew 'em up."

Eisenhower stepped on Patton's exuberance by stating firmly that the Germans could not be allowed to cross the Meuse. Mostly because of the confused situation and meager reports from the front, the seriousness of the situation was not fully appreciated by those attending this meeting. It was determined, however, that the northern sector of the Bulge should be bolstered by the movement south of some First and Ninth Army forces and, while this flank held the German advance, Patton should swing strong elements of his Third Army to the north and head for Bastogne. Patton confidently predicted that he could wheel ninety degrees, move the hundred miles over the narrow, icy roads and be ready to attack the flanks of the German penetration within forty-eight hours.

By the following day, December 20, it became apparent how serious the situation was. The deep wedge driven into the Allied lines had split Bradley's command (the 12th Army Group, consisting of the First, Third, and Ninth Armies), and there was little or no communication between his 12th Army Group headquarters in Luxembourg and Hodges's First Army headquarters, Chaudfontaine. Neither was there any satisfactory liaison between the severed sections of the First Army itself.

Eisenhower, partial to Bradley as a friend and confident in him as a commander, now made what for him must have been one of the most difficult decisions of the war. He put all forces north of the Bulge under Montgomery's leadership. Thus, on the twentieth of December, the whole of Simpson's United States Ninth Army and most of Hodges's United States First Army was placed under Montgomery's control. Bradley was left with a few battered divisions of the First south of the Bulge and Patton's Third Army, three divisions of which were heading pell-mell for Bastogne.

Montgomery ordered General Matthew Ridgway's 18th Airborne Corps to drive southwest to the aid of the 7th Armored Division, still defending a twenty-five-mile horseshoe-shaped area around St.-Vith, and then to proceed to Bastogne. Ridgway, with one combat command of the 3rd Armored and all of the crack 82nd Airborne, drove forward through crumbling elements of other United States units.

"That whole Ardennes fight was a battle of road junctions," General Ridgway said, "because in the wooded country, in the deep snows, armies could not move off the roads. . . . I remember [one incident] with regret," the unbending Ridgway recalled. "The Germans had brought up some flat trajectory guns, and they started shelling our little group. Fragments whizzed everywhere. One struck an artillery observer, who was standing by me, in the leg, and another punctured the tank of his jeep. As this shell exploded, an infantry sergeant standing nearby became hysterical. He threw himself into the ditch by the side of the road, crying and raving. I walked over and tried to talk to him, trying to help him get hold of himself. But it had no effect. He was just crouched there in the ditch, cringing in utter terror. So I called my jeep driver, Sergeant Farmer, and told him to take his carbine and march this man back to the nearest M.P., and if he started to escape to shoot him without hesitation. He was an object of abject cowardice, and the sight of him would have had a terrible effect on any American soldier who might see him.

". . . It is an appalling thing to witness—to see a man break completely like that—in battle. It is worse than watching a death —for you are seeing something more important than the body die. You are witnessing the death of a man's spirit, of his pride, of all that gives meaning and purpose to life."

For every man who cracked in the Battle of the Bulge and sank to the lower depths of his emotions, there was another who rose to the upper range of his. Thousands of men discovered under pressure of war that they possessed capacities for accomplishment that they had never used and these men, extending themselves now, became heroic. They carried with them the great number of men who were neither cowardly nor aggressively brave. Lieutenant Eric Wood was one of these heroes.

A former Princeton fullback with a wife and two children at home, Wood was up front with one of the artillery battalions hardest hit when the German push started. Wood's battery commander was killed, and most of the men were captured. Wood waited; and as the advance panzer tanks approached his position three abreast, he coolly destroyed one and sent the other two in hasty, if temporary, retreat. Wood then got three of his heavy howitzers out of the deep snow and muck and fell back with them down the northwestern slopes of the Schnee Eifel ridge. Wood's three-piece "battalion" beat the Germans to the bridge over the Our River by minutes, and took up a position protecting the left flank of the advancing 82nd Airborne. When the battery was finally forced to move, Wood took them down the road towards the town of Schoenberg. Over the brow of a small hill, Wood's big truck, pulling the bouncing howitzer behind it, came face to face with a German Tiger tank. You can't back up a truck pulling an artillery piece, and the howitzer was facing to the rear. Wood's driver jammed on the brakes and the twelve-man gun crew fell to the ditch by the side of the road seconds before the Tiger's 88 blasted the truck into small parts. The tank moved up, and Wehrmacht infantry started forward. Wood's gun crew surrendered in the near hopeless situation and, as the Germans approached warily, the men were surprised to see one of their ranks bound for the woods. German riflemen splattered bullets off the trees kicking up the snow behind the fleeing American, Lieutenant Eric Wood.

Wood made his way to the little town of Meyerode, four miles north of where he had lost his last gun and gun crew. In town that night he was given food and a good featherbed to sleep in

by the townspeople. As he prepared to leave next morning, they warned him that the area between Meyerode and St.-Vith was full of Germans.

Wood shrugged off the dangers: "I'll either fight my way back to my outfit or I'll collect some American stragglers and start a small war of my own."

Wood did just that: for the next three days he fought his own guerrilla war in the woods near Meyerode. The Germans moved into the village in strength the next day and every time a small force of them tried to move through the narrow mountain roads, they reached Meyerode with several dead and wounded. Often as not they had abandoned several burning vehicles destroyed by this mysterious fire from the woods.

The specific circumstances under which Eric Wood died are not known. Late in January, after the Germans were beaten back, his body was found in the forest. With him lay seven dead Germans. He had fought to the end.

Wood was not the average American soldier, nor was the boy that Ridgway found whimpering in terror by the side of the road.

COUNTERING THE COUNTERATTACK

Despite the fact that Ridgway's Airborne outfit made contact with Hasbrouck's 7th Armored forces defending St.-Vith, that city finally fell on December 21, five days behind von Rundstedt's timetable. This left Bastogne the lone island of resistance, as panzer units flowed around and past it in their drive to the Meuse. Montgomery ordered General Ernest Harmon ("Old Gravel Throat") to move his 2nd Armored Division south from its position near Aachen to a point near Havelange, seventy miles southwest, directly in the path of the deepest German penetration. Harmon got his orders late on the afternoon of December 21.

There were about fourteen thousand men in an armored division. They moved in three hundred wheeled vehicles and about five hundred tanks. If they maintained the regulation Army distance of fifty yards between vehicles, an armored division in single file made a column more than one hundred miles long.

Harmon's column started to move at midnight on the twenty-first, and by 11:30 the following morning the leading elements of the strong division were in Havelange, directly in the path of the German front runners.

"We used sixty thousand gallons of gas," Harmon said, "but we arrived ready for battle. Only eleven vehicles failed to make the full march. They had slipped off the icy roads or had engine failures."

Montgomery had ordered Harmon to sit still with his 2nd Armored and make no contact with the enemy. The division's presence in the Germans' path was to be a surprise; but while Harmon and his staff officers were relaxing over lunch, waiting for further orders after their forced march from Aachen, a bandaged and bloody lieutenant demanded entrance to the dining room of the château at Havelange. This frantic messenger, Lieutenant Everett Jones, hurriedly told Harmon of a pitched battle he and his small reconnaissance outfit had fought with a strong German force a few miles away near the town of Haid. Jones's force had abandoned most of their vehicles, and Harmon realized the presence of the 2nd Armored was no longer a secret to the Germans.

For the next five days, the 2nd Armored locked horns with the 2nd Panzer Division and elements of the 9th Panzer. Eventually, it was the proud panzer division that cracked—but after five days of bitter fighting.

It began to seem as though every time things looked better for the American forces, things got worse. The 30th Division retook Stavelot in some of the war's most vicious fighting, but farther south the Germans threw twelve new divisions through the breach, gaining ground and taking a heavy toll of United States forces. Everywhere a United States division was sent in to attack, it found itself on the defensive. The three divisions Patton had swung north to strike at the flank of the German penetration made a stunning march and attacked, as he had said they would, within forty-eight hours from the time they were ordered to move. Inside Bastogne, McAuliffe was elated at the news of their swift change of direction. It appeared as though they could provide the relief he needed so desperately. The 4th Armored was headed directly for Bastogne, the veteran 80th under General "Hairless Horace" McBride was on the east, or right flank of the move, and the green 26th Division—composed mostly of some barrel-scrapings made from various service units behind Paris—was aimed at neighboring Wiltz. Unfortunately for McAuliffe and the men inside Bastogne, the Germans had monitored the radio network directing the Third Army move, and they were braced for this attack on their open side. Patton was temporarily foiled in his plan to smash through to Bastogne in one quick stroke.

By December 24, it became apparent to the German General Staff that despite some success they could not accomplish their major objective, the taking of Antwerp. They decided instead to drive to Dinant, on the west bank of the Meuse, and then sweep north of Aachen. Another force was to push west across the Roer River. When these two German columns met, they would have large elements of the United States First and Ninth Armies cut off.

To accomplish this plan and to reach Dinant, it was vital to the Germans that Bastogne be cleared of the stubborn American forces there. To this end, the 15th Panzer Grenadier Division was moved to the northwest edge of the Bastogne perimeter. German tanks had already perforated the defenses once, and had actually rolled into the streets of Bastogne before being driven back. The Germans estimated that the crushing force provided by the addition of the 15th Panzer Grenadier would enable them to swamp the defenders.

They picked the wrong defenders to try to swamp.

On Christmas Eve, the men in Bastogne knew something big was coming at them and they were ready to fight—but hardly confident. Air supplies had continued to reach them in good amounts, but they knew they were greatly outnumbered. After the early evening bombing by the Luftwaffe, which was rela-

A few civilians will not leave their battered town.

tively ineffective, the Germans starting applying pressure to their nutcracker. Their tanks and infantry jumped off at 3 A.M. Christmas morning, and by dawn they had punched a narrow hole through the ring of Bastogne defenders to the northwest. Eighteen heavy German tanks trundled through this gap, accompanied by several hundred infantrymen. McAuliffe, realizing in advance where the German attack was coming, had placed tank destroyers in strategic locations; by eleven o'clock Christmas morning all eighteen German tanks had been destroyed, and no German infantryman escaped. By noon the American ring around Bastogne was intact again.

Things were looking up for the Battered Bastards. On the twenty-sixth the Germans made one last, desperate push to storm the city, but as they came in from the northwest, a combat command of the 4th Armored Division broke through the German lines diagonally across the ring, and rushed to add their fresh strength to that of the embattled 10th Armored and 101st Airborne. This was the happy ending to the glorious defense of Bastogne, and it immortalized McAuliffe's curt "Nuts!" (McAuliffe has spent much of his postwar life denying that his answer was anything less printable.)

THE HOLE IS PLUGGED

The German 2nd Panzer Division, and elements of the 9th Panzer and Panzer Lehr, were crushed by Harmon's 2nd Armored. The Germans, unaware that the 2nd had moved from Aachen, were struck full force on their northern flank as well as from directly west; these elite divisions of Hitler's were massacred in the snows around Rochefort and Celles. The Germans, short of gas, made pillboxes of their tanks. The panzer armored units were often better armed and more heavily armored than the American divisions with their Shermans, but they were not nearly so mobile. United States tank crews often complained that they were not as well protected with armor plate as the Germans, nor were their 75 mm guns a match for the German 88s. It turned out, however, that the American vehicles won almost every tank-to-tank duel. They could move over snow and mush that trapped the heavier panzer tanks, and while their guns were not so big, the German tank rifle was traversed and brought into firing position by a gunner turning a heavy geared wheel. The Sherman's guns were equipped with electric motors that automatically moved the artillery piece quickly onto the selected target. Often the American tankers got off three quick blasts before the enemy gunner could bring his piece into firing position. And three was usually enough.

Christmas and the day after marked the turning point in the Battle of the Bulge, although for the men fighting things did not seem much different. American soldiers were dying moving forward instead of backward. With the linkup of the 4th Armored and the besieged forces at Bastogne, the 17th Airborne, the 11th Armored and the 87th Infantry Divisions were added to Patton's Third Army, attacking the German spearhead from below. On January 3 Montgomery initiated a drive at the base of the German Bulge, from the north. The 84th Infantry Division teamed with the 2nd Armored, and the 83rd worked with the 3rd Armored. The air had cleared and the tenuous German columns stretching through the Ardennes were being attacked regularly now by the Air Force.

Von Rundstedt tried to convince Hitler that they should pull back immediately and form a new defensive line.

"I am convinced," Hitler said, "that in the long run we cannot maintain the defensive. Only the offensive will enable us to give a successful turn to the war in the west."

Patton now had six divisions attacking the German flank from the south. On January 1, Hitler, still determined to drive through Bastogne and reach the Meuse, launched a minor offensive with eight divisions in the Saar, the area from which he assumed Patton had drawn his strength. His object was to force the Third Army to withdraw its forces from the Ardennes salient to meet the new German thrust.

At about the same time, the Luftwaffe staged its last great operation of the war. In memory of its great days when the Stukas

were terrifying enemy troops with their dive-bombing, eight hundred German Air Force planes swooped down on a dozen Allied airfields in Belgium and Holland in a desperate attempt to crush the United States and British air elements that were bedeviling their road and rail movements. This Luftwaffe attack damaged or destroyed about 250 Allied aircraft, but there were more where they came from; the Luftwaffe lost 200 planes, and they were irreplaceable.

Although it had seemed as though the battle of Bastogne were over when the 4th Armored entered the city, on the 3rd and 4th of January the Germans launched their heaviest offensive against it. Bastogne, no longer surrounded, was well defended; despite the great pressure from eight German divisions, it once more held out.

Although less dramatic, this second battle for Bastogne was more costly in men and material than the first. With many of Hitler's SS troops in the attack and with tough United States paratroopers facing them at many points, it was a dirty fight. The Germans booby-trapped the dead and dying, and the snow, heavy on the ground now, provided a quick easy place for hiding mines. The story of the Malmédy Massacre had spread through the Allied Army, and American soldiers found themselves with a personal hatred and desire to kill that they had not previously held. American soldiers were united by this common emotion of hatred and fought together as they rarely had before.

The German defeat at Bastogne became complete on January 9 and United States forces from the north, augmented by elements of the British XXX Corps, pushed for Houffalize as the Third Army moved north past Bastogne. On January 12 the Russians, the pressure on their front greatly eased by the shifting of German strength to the west, began their last great offensive, which was to carry them eventually to Berlin. Hitler frantically moved the Sixth SS Panzer Army across Germany to face the new threat from the east; on January 16, the 84th Division from the Hodges

Americans massacred at Malmédy are numbered for identification.

First Army and the 11th Armored from the Patton Third Army met in Houffalize. The Bulge was pinched off.

"The Battle of the Bulge," said Winston Churchill, "was the greatest American battle of the war."

The official end of the battle came on January 28, when the Germans were shoved back to their original positions.

That day the German General Staff issued this statement:

THIS, WESTERN WARRIORS, WAS YOUR ACHIEVEMENT. YOU HAVE TRANSCENDED ALL DIFFICULTIES OF TERRAIN AND WEATHER TO PROVE THAT YOU ARE TOUGHER THAN THE ENEMY. YOUR LEADERS AND YOUR COUNTRY KNOW THAT THEY CAN PLACE THEIR FAITH IN YOU. THE ENEMY WAS FORCED TO COMMIT ALL HIS RESERVES . . . THE INTENDED ALLIED ASSAULT TOWARD COLOGNE AND THE RUHR WAS MADE IMPOSSIBLE. THE DANGER OF A WESTERN OFFENSIVE, CO-ORDINATED WITH THE HUGE BOLSHEVIST DRIVE, WAS AVERTED.

This was whistling in the dark. The German position, although they held the same line, was substantially worse than it had been on December 16. The Allied attack had been delayed six weeks, but German morale and the will to fight was gone. They had inflicted a total of 76,000 casualties on the United States forces, but they themselves had lost 100,000, and 30,000 of these were dead. Some of Hitler's best divisions had been destroyed beyond the German capacity to rebuild them. The Battle of the Bulge was the last great fight in Europe. The broken Germans began surrendering in such numbers that feeding them was a greater problem than fighting them. Six weeks later, the war in Europe was over.

It was the Russians who profited most by the Germans' Ardennes offensive. When they struck on January 12, the best German divisions were occupied in the west. They swept across Poland and were able to beat out Allied forces in the race for Berlin.

Bastogne, while not the most important engagement in the battle, has become a symbol of the tenacity with which American soldiers fought off Adolf Hitler's one last, wild charge to conquer the world.

PICTURE SOURCES

Defense Department, U.S. Marine Corps

pp. 10–11, 14–15, 18–19, 25, 26, 28–29, 32–33, 36–37, 40–41, 46–47

U.S. Army

pp. 21, 39, 52–53, 91, 120–21, 125, 129, 130–131, 132, 137, 140–141, 144, 148–149, 154–155, 159, 170–171, 174–175, 176–177, 184, 190–191, 194, 204–205, 207, 211, 214–215, 216, 220–221, 222–223, 227, 228–229, 232–233, 236–237, 238–239, 240–241

Sovfoto

pp. 57, 60–61, 63, 64, 66–67, 68, 71, 72–73, 74–75, 78–79, 82–83, 92, 96–97, 108–109, 110–111

Herman Axelbank

pp. 102, 104–105

Robert Capa-Magnum

pp. 116–117, 166–167, 168–169, 197

U.S. Coast Guard

pp. 161, 162–163, 180–181

book design by Betty Binns